The Care and Repair of

FISHING TACKLE

The Care and Repair of
FISHING TACKLE

MEL MARSHALL

Photographs by the author and Aldine Marshall

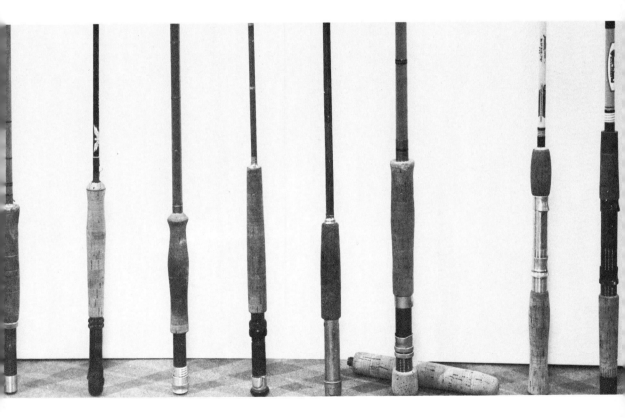

WINCHESTER PRESS

Library of Congress Cataloging in Publication Data
Marshall, Mel.
    The care and repair of fishing tackle.
    Includes index.
    1. Fishing tackle—Maintenance and repair. I. Title.
SH447.M37   688.7'9   76-22569
ISBN 0-87691-183-1

Published by Winchester Press, Inc.
205 East 42nd Street, New York, N.Y. 10017

Printed in the United States of America

CONTENTS

ACKNOWLEDGMENTS

Credit for much material in this book goes to a lot of people.

My thanks to the fishing tackle manufacturers whose replies to questionnaires covering various aspects of the industry made valuable data available, and to the American Fishing Tackle Manufacturers Association for assistance in circulating the questionnaire.

Special thanks to the firms responding to requests for out-of-the-ordinary information about their products and to those providing items for examination, experimenting, and photo use: Allan Tackle Manufacturing Co., Auto-Gaff, Browning, Cortland Line Co., Daiwa, Fenwick, Gudebrod Bros., Quick Corporation of America, Roy System Shoes, Scientific Anglers, Shakespeare Co., Varmac Manufacturing Co., and Fritz von Schlegell.

Friends old and new, acquaintances, and strangers both in and outside the tackle industry helped in many ways. My thanks to Harry Argovitz, Manny Beardsley, R. Q. Biggers, Tom Brennan, J. L. Chandler, Rex Gerlach, Bob Hills, George Hine, Fred Hooven, Bob Jack, Bill Jacobs, Eveline Leonard, Bob Lewis, John Merchant, Rich Miller, Morris Mitchell, Jim Murray, Dave Myers, Verna Nagel, Fred Northrup, Norm Pflug, Bob Phillip, Donald Rienzo, Buck Smith, Tom Wicker, George Uyeno, Fritz von Schlegell, and John Zervas. If I've overlooked or forgotten others who helped, I'm sorry.

ACKNOWLEDGMENTS

Most of all, I'm deeply indebted to fishing companions of present and past years who passed on to me tricks they'd learned and a lot of tricks they originated. Some of these men were angling veterans when I was a novice, and a few had begun fishing before I was born; these shared with me their experiences and memories of days when tackle was primitive, fishermen were few, and all streams ran clear and were full of fish.

M.M.

The Care and Repair of

FISHING TACKLE

1

WHY BOTHER?

During the 1950s and 1960s, if you'd picked a hundred fishermen at random and asked how much maintenance or home repair work they did on their tackle, more than half of them would have replied, "Why bother? If I break something or a piece of my gear wears out, I just throw it away and buy something new." If the same hundred fishermen were asked the same question now, the percentage of those following the "throw it away, buy a new one" approach to fishing tackle would be found to have dwindled dramatically.

Changed times bring changed attitudes. When the prices of almost everything began rising during the 1960s and were still spiraling upward fifteen years later, we began altering our attitudes toward all our belongings, from cars and appliances and tools right on down to the equipment we use in recreational activities. By the early 1970s, most of us were willing to return to the old hard-times Yankee philosophy of "fix it up, make it do."

Fishing tackle prices were pulled up not only by the worldwide inflation and money devaluations that began in the 1950s, but also by an entirely new and unexpectedly huge generation of fishermen created by increasing leisure time and expansion of good fishing waters. Between 1945–1965, over 5,000 new lakes, ponds, and reservoirs stocked with fish were opened to a recreation-hungry public. Fishing became a family sport, and as the beginning fishermen grew more and more expert, they began demanding better, more complicated tackle that cost more to produce. Even without the inflationary pressures that increased costs of materials, labor, power, and so on, the changed demands of fishermen would have sent prices upward.

What might be described as the modern innovative period of tackle design had been interrupted by World War II. Until well into the 1930s, fishing equipment had largely been handcrafted in small shops rather than mass-produced in factories, and even today there are a substantial number of tackle manufacturers with plants that are small by modern industrial standards. To a large extent, making fishing tackle is still pretty much of a handicraft as opposed to a computerized, automated assembly-line operation.

Surface similarities tend to hide the fact that most modern fishing tackle has little except appearance and function in common with yesterday's gear. Many, perhaps most, of these differences resulted originally from shortages of traditional tackle-making materials. The first fiberglass rods were created to substitute for the bamboo that was a World War II casualty; silk, another wartime victim, was replaced by synthetic fibers; tough new plastics originated for use in place of scarce metals have resulted in lighter, more compact reels. A whole new family of tackle was born when veterans returning from Europe wanted spinning gear, until the 1950s virtually unknown in the U.S.

As increasingly sophisticated anglers began demanding more versatile, more easily used tackle, manufacturers moved to fill these demands. A baitcasting reel of the 1950s vintage typically had as few as fifteen to twenty components; by the 1970s, full-function baitcasting reels require from seventy-five to one hundred high-precision components, and the cost of making and assembling such reels has quite naturally gone up. This change is reflected in virtually every item of angling gear.

While the availability of inexpensive fishing gear did encourage new fishermen to adopt the sport, it also encouraged them to acquire bad tackle habits. When less time and only a little more expense was involved, it was easier to replace a broken or damaged rod or reel with a new one then to repair the broken item. There was little incentive to fix a broken $8 rod when a brand-new one could be bought at that price, or a broken $10 reel could be replaced with its new $10 twin. Discarding and replacing has become less frequent now that the rod that yesterday cost $10 has disappeared and a new one of comparable quality costs $25, and when the reel that once cost $15 can only be replaced with a new one priced at twice that much.

Of course, there has always been a number of anglers who did tackle-tinkering for the sheer pleasure of it. Some found it a way to extend the fishing season; when weather or the calendar closed streams and lakes, there was a favorite rod to fit with new guides or a new grip, or a reel with frozen gears, or lures that needed renovating. A lot of these tackle-tinkerers were moved less by the idea of saving money than they were by the prospect of working with items that recalled happy hours outdoors. Others found a challenge in equaling or even surpassing the work done by the original maker of a piece of gear. A few took up the hobby because it gave them a chance to modify or personalize a piece of factory-made equipment by adding to it distinctive, individual touches of their own.

Certainly the heritage carried over from an earlier era of angling, when virtually every item of a fisherman's equipment was hand made, must have led many to take up tackle-tinkering. Although today we tend to look on much early tackle as quaint, even antique, let's remember that handmade split-bamboo rods weren't superseded by factory-made rods until the late 1920s; that reels were made in shops instead of factories until about 1910; that lines were hand laid well into the 1930s; and that mass-production of plugs and metal lures did not begin until early in the twentieth century.

Many of the angling innovations that benefit us today are little more than a century old. They did not originate, as do today's new ideas, in the design room of a manufacturer, but resulted from inquisitive trial-and-error experiments and adaptations by amateurs. Some of the best-known firms in today's fishing tackle industry in both the United States and Europe still bear the names of the tackle-tinkering amateur anglers who founded them. A substantial number are still family enterprises. For the most part, the men who founded the modern fishing-tackle industry were less concerned originally with creating commercially valuable products than they were in making their own fishing hours more productive and pleasant.

Anglers addicted to the "throw it away, buy something new" approach are still around. There will always be the lazy or careless fisherman who neglects such simple routine jobs as stripping and cleaning a reel to get rid of abrasive sand and grit and to renew the lubricants that will keep its performance perfect and prolong its useful life. There will always be those who put off replacing the frayed windings on a guide until the guide pops off while a heavy fish is being played and the unnatural strain placed on the rod tip causes it to fracture. Inevitably, a percentage of good and usable tackle is still going to be tossed onto the junk heap.

Converts to the philosophy of maintaining and repairing their fishing gear often feel handicapped, hampered by lack of knowledge of even basic maintenance routines and simple repair jobs. Instruction booklets that manufacturers provide with new equipment have all too often been glanced at, tossed aside, or misplaced, their contents forgotten. Faced with a broken piece of equipment, a lot of fishermen are reluctant to try repairing it because they think they will have to acquire new tools and learn new skills.

One result of the growing number of "fix-it-up" converts, combined with hesitancy about taking on the fix-up jobs themselves, has been a flood of work flowing to tackle-repair shops. During the "throw it away, buy a new one" era, independent repair facilities dwindled—they were never numerous—and factory-repair facilities became faced with a volume of work that was unexpectedly large. While factory-repair shops were being enlarged and expanded, and new service technicians trained, the tackle-repair business got a reputation for slow and sluggish work and sent to local shops a flood of repair jobs with which the shops weren't prepared to cope.

Virtually every fishing tackle manufacturer in the United States has expanded and enlarged its service facilities since 1970, and many have extended their operations to include regional and local shops manned by trained servicemen. The day of the six-month wait for tackle repairs has passed, but service facilities still tend to center, quite naturally, around established fishing areas and in the bigger cities.

In gathering material for this book, I surveyed all the leading U.S. tackle manufacturers, and learned that the manufacturers whose sales are greatest in volume receive from 60,000 to 100,000 rods and reels for repair each year. Manufacturers who produce lines confined to a dozen rod and reel models instead of the thirty or more made by the bigger firms report handling from 8,000 to 25,000 repair jobs annually. The repair volume of a few specialized manufacturers will run to only 500 to 800 jobs a year.

A similar survey of retail tackle dealers in widely separated geographical areas proved more difficult to analyze statistically. In locations where good fishing opportunities have been available over a long period of time, tackle stores are understandably more numerous, their operators more experienced, and their staffing is usually planned to include individuals qualified to handle repair work. In areas where fishing opportunities are less abundant and tackle stores smaller and less numerous, there may only be a part-time repair worker, or perhaps none at all. In these smaller stores, however, it's common for the operator to have an arrangement by which an outside independent contractor will handle the store's repair work.

Local shops will usually handle simple repairs such as replacing a rod tip-top or guide while the customer waits, but more complex repairs will take three to five days. Factory-repair shops require from one to twenty-eight days to repair a rod or reel, the median being eleven days. The shortest time quoted was 24 hours, which was given by 30 percent of my respondents; the longest was two to four weeks, quoted by 10 percent of those replying. The other 60 percent quoted periods ranging from four to eight days. Remember, these are actual in-shop times, and doesn't include the time your equipment spends in the mail traveling to and from the factory shop.

Tackle manufacturers as a group are very conscious of their service departments. With only one or two exceptions, the firms surveyed noted that their repair facilities have been enlarged and improved in recent years, and in some instances are still being expanded. However, the manufacturers face the same problem that plagues a fisherman needing a rod or reel repair job: there just aren't enough skilled, trained tackle repairmen to fill the need, and often the first step a manufacturer wanting to expand service facilities must take is to train people to do the work.

One reason for this book is to tell you in words and pictures how to take care of the repair jobs most often needed to restore a rod, reel, or other gear to normal use. But it also tells you which jobs should be referred to an expert. Most of the repairs covered can be handled with the tools that will generally be found in any home: screwdrivers, pliers, adjustable wrench, hacksaw, hammer, and small electric drill. Whenever a job can be done more quickly and with less trouble using specialized tools, this will be noted, but in most cases a substitute will also be suggested.

I have a special drawer in my workshop reserved for the special-purpose tools I've bought and used only once. It took a while for the realization to soak in that it's silly to buy an internal pipe wrench when you might need one only once in ten or fifteen years, and this applies to almost any limited-use tool. It just doesn't make sense to buy any special-purpose tool for a one-time job, unless that tool costs less than a couple of bucks. Besides, most such tools require specially acquired skills to be used efficiently, while the tools you use regularly fit easily into your hands.

However, if you have the dual objective of learning how to repair fishing tackle while at the same time adding to your tool collection, there's an appendix to the book that gives you the sources of supply for just about any tool you've ever heard of, including internal pipe wrenches.

Anybody who's skillful enough to learn how to cast with a rod and reel can quickly master the skills needed to maintain and repair that rod and reel. Reels present the greatest confusion to the amateur repairman, but needn't, because there are remarkable similarities of construction in almost all brands of reels. Once you're acquainted with them, the innards of baitcasting, spinning, spincasting, and fly reels are pretty much alike. Rods, of course, are even more uniform in their basic components, whether they're the all-prevalent hollow fiberglass, or the new High Modulus Graphite (HMG) or the increasingly less-common solid fiberglass rods.

Like all handcrafted articles, new bamboo rods are in limited supply, and high in price, which is all the more reason for giving the best of care to any good bamboo rod you might have. There are, incidentally, quite a few good old bamboo rods tucked away gathering dust and cobwebs in attics and storerooms. Many of these rods still have a lot of useful life left in them, and with just a bit of work can be put in usable condition, ready to give you many hours of pleasant use. Since there's very little literature currently available on bamboo rods, the chapter covering rods has a special section dealing with bamboos.

A lot of other items of fishing gear have gone up in price to the point where repairing and refurbishing them is more practical than buying replacements. Lines, for example, can often be rebuilt to remove cracked spots in the finish; this isn't as important with monofilament lines as it is with $15 to $25 fly lines. Both plug and metal lures that have gotten battered can be revived with buffing compound, paint, tape, new hooks, and hardware. Creels, nets, waders, boots—practically every item in an angler's array of equipment—respond to treatment, if you're interested in taking the time and willing to make the effort.

Willingness to make the effort is perhaps the greatest key to your success in maintaining and repairing your own tackle. Most of the items used in fishing are designed to be easy to maintain and simple to repair, and in 99.9 percent of all cases, no special tool is needed. But you must be interested in doing this for pleasure, not as a disliked chore, or you're whipped before you start. Sure, you'll get your hands dirty, but no dirtier than they'd get in cleaning a fish. Sure, you'll put out a little effort, but no more effort than you'd spend wading a stream all day after hiking two hours to reach it.

Certainly you'll need some special know-how, and this book provides the information needed to go about virtually any job of repairing and maintaining your tackle. I've tried to provide it in a way that will save even the beginner from making false starts and traveling up blind alleys. There are going to be times when lack of maintenance has reduced a rod or reel to a condition that makes futile any effort to repair or restore it. Occasionally, you'll accidentally smash a piece of equipment so badly that it will be past fixing, at least by a professional repairman's standards. But often an amateur tackle-tinkerer can successfully complete a job that a professional would refuse, because he'd be forced to charge more for his time and the necessary parts than the replacement cost of the item. Not being required to set a cash value on your time, working at repairing tackle as a relaxing hobby, you can often restore a piece of gear at very small expense and profit not only by getting continued use from it, but from the satisfaction of knowing you've done a good job.

I learned an important lesson from a baitcasting rod that today has more value as an antique than it did when it was first made about 1910 or 1911 by E. F. Payne. The rod was snagged by a big wet fly that I was fishing on the bottom of a mountain lake. The reel that was still attached to the rod had rusted beyond repair or salvage, but the rod was still being held together by its ferrule, tip-top, and a guide or two. Prolonged immersion had frozen the ferrule between its two sections, and water had dissolved the varnish that once had protected it as well as the glue that had held its five bamboo strips together. Underwater, the bamboo had swelled and bulged, snapping most of the guide wraps, but the cork grip and German silver reel seat were undamaged.

My first reaction was to toss the rod back into the lake, but after a close inspection and a little rubbing disclosed the Payne name stamped on the reel seat, I became curious. The lake I was fishing was the central feature of a resort that had been in operation since the early 1800s, and I thought perhaps one of the old-timers who still visited the place might be able to tell me something of the rod's history. Sure enough, one could. I learned that the rod and reel had been dropped from a boat by the long-dead minister who'd owned them. The minister had been a regular visitor to the resort, and my informant remembered how angry and chagrined the preacher had been when he'd accidentally lost his prized rod overboard at some time in the early 1920s. I found the rod in the late 1940s, so it had rested on the bottom for more than a quarter-century.

Learning its story prompted me to take the rod home after discarding the useless reel. Eventually, I got the idea of having it restored, and took it to Abercrombie & Fitch, who were dealers for Payne rods. The A&F people agreed to show the rod to Jim Payne, son of Ed, on his next visit to the store, and get his opinion as to the feasibility of restoring it. They did so, and recounted to me in great detail the careful examination, the dating of the rod's crafting as 1910 or 1911, and the sad verdict by Jim Payne that to restore the rod would be prohibitively costly and probably wouldn't result in it being usable even if restored.

Having made a few bamboo rods, I knew the judgment was fair and honest. I really didn't want to use the rod for fishing, but still couldn't bring myself to junk what had originally been an example of fine craftsmanship by one of America's pioneer rodmakers. I began the job of restoration, putting in twenty minutes, a half hour, whenever I was free to do so. Over a period of several months, I restored the rod to its original condition, using the same grip, reel seat, and ferrules with which it was first equipped and even scrounged up a set of agate guides to match those left on it. When I'd finished, the rod looked as though it had just come off Payne's workbench, and the grain of its fine bamboo seen through a shining coat of varnish is still a delight to the eye.

I share the story of the Payne rod with you to make a point: Most items of fishing tackle can be restored or repaired by an amateur who's willing to take the time and trouble. It's a lot easier to keep your tackle in good condition by giving it proper care and maintenance, but if you have gear that needs attention, it can probably be put into good shape again. Perhaps the information in the chapters that follow will give you the confidence to take on jobs that until now you've thought were too complicated for an amateur. Perhaps there will be some shortcuts you haven't yet discovered in both maintaining and repairing your equipment. Perhaps there will be information that will save you from starting a project, only to find after you've gone to a lot of trouble and expense that the job is one best left to a professional. And, if you're one of the holdovers who still shrugs and asks, "Why bother?" when the subject of maintenance and repairs to tackle comes up in your angling chats, you might even find some information here that will cause you to change your mind and to discover for yourself the very real pleasures of tackle-tinkering.

2

RODS

Since angling history began to be recorded, fishermen have been experimenting with a wide variety of materials in search of the ideal substance from which to fabricate fishing rods. Such a substance would produce a rod that is light in weight; strong when formed into a long, thin wandlike shape; sensitive in transmitting vibrations created by the slightest touch of a line attached to the rod; flexibly elastic; capable of being bent into a resilient arc that will straighten immediately; tough in its resistance to crushing or to sudden sharp blows; and pleasing to look at. So far, the absolutely ideal substance has still to be discovered or invented. But let's take a look at some of those that have been and are being used.

Fishing rods were probably discovered accidentally when some prehistoric angler tied his baited handline to a bush or tree branch overhanging a stream. Let's call this prehistoric fisherman Ghu. After tying his handline to the branch, Ghu lay down for a streamside nap, and woke to a rustle of leaves caused by a fish tugging at the line, which caused the branch to sway up and down. Ghu noted how effectively the springy branch tamed the plunging fish without breaking the primitive line of woven bark threads, and the next time he fished, Ghu broke off a branch that he held in his hand after tying his line to its tip. Ghu's descendants are not only the young country lads whose rods are willow branches, but the still-sizable army of cane-pole fishermen.

Made-up rods date back to ancient Egypt, where tomb pictures that are believed to have been painted as long as 3,500 years ago show anglers using long slim rods made by lashing together calamus or horunda reeds. Some of the figures pictured holding these rods are royal or noble, so fishing as a sport is of great antiquity.

By the fifteenth century B.C., strip-built rods had evolved. These were made from carefully chosen sections taken from limbs of hardwood trees such as oak and hickory. The sections were shaved into long tapered triangular-shaped lengths, fitted smoothly together, and bound with strips of wet rawhide to form a rod of 16 to 20 feet long; when the rawhide strips dried, they shrank to hold the pieces of wood firmly together. Sometime during the middle of the eighteenth century, English and Scottish gamekeepers began using such exotic woods as greenheart and ironwood, from which rods of smaller diameter (and consequently more sensitivity) could be made. By no stretch of the imagination could such rods be called light; a 20-foot rod was weighed in pounds, not ounces.

Bamboo first came into use in the waning days of the eighteenth century. Daniel Rogan, a British veteran of Indian service who had turned gamekeeper, is credited with having learned bamboo crafting while in India; Rogan is believed to have made the first bamboo rods as early as 1796. In that era, a fisherman did not cast in today's sense of the word, since the rods they used were not equipped with guides that would allow a line to slip through easily. The guides used were of the type called "ring and keeper," and as you can see from the accompanying picture, the loose ring flopping around in its "keeper" would impede rather than encourage a line to flow through it freely.

In actual use, the chief value of the ring and keeper guides was that the fisherman had much more freedom to play a fish than was possible when the line was fastened securely to the tip of the rod. And, with a 20-foot rod plus a line equal in length to that of the rod, a fisherman could make a cast of 40 feet, usually enough to reach the unsophisticated fish of those early days when the fish in a given stretch of stream outnumbered the anglers on its banks. Casting as we know it today began developing only after 1830, when an Irish gillie named Malloch invented a rigid guide through which a line would run freely,

"Ring and keeper" guides must have been frustrating to fish with. The loose flopping ring through which the line passed would not only twist in its keeper, but would push a wet line down and encourage it to cling to the rod.

and Frederic Halford developed lines to match the capability of the rods that were fitted with the new guides.

Bamboo dominated rodmaking for more than a century, until World War II. The best bamboo, known as Tonkin cane, came from an area roughly 150 miles square, lying to the north of Canton, China, but there was to be no more Tonkin cane shipped to U.S. and European rodmakers for more than thirty years. Rodmakers turned to metals, spring steel, and alloys such as beryllium-copper; not only were metal rods heavy and inflexible, they fractured and cracked quickly under the internal stresses created by repeated casting. Metal was quickly abandoned once fiberglass appeared on the scene.

By the late 1930s a process of extruding molten glass through microscopically small holes to form long filaments had been evolved.

Bundles of these filaments, when imbedded in a plastic, produced a very flexible cylinder; the degree of flexibility of these cylinders could be controlled by varying the plastic-to-glass ratio, or by using filaments of different diameters, or by using different types of plastic for the embedment. When ground on a centerless grinder into a taper, these cylinders became the blanks on which the first generation of glass rods was made.

These early solid glass rods had more flaws than virtues. They were heavy in feel and either overstiff or overwhippy in action, and after being used for a relatively short time tended to break down. This was because at that period there was not enough technical knowledge of plastics composition to produce a material that would bond perfectly with glass. After repeated flexing while being cast, the fibers that had been shortened when the rod was ground to its taper began to pop free of the plastic in which they were imbedded. This not only produced an unpleasant prickly fuzz on the rod's surface, but created weak spots that cracked in a circle around the rod, which soon broke into two or more pieces.

Later, it became possible to produce plastics that bonded the glass filaments perfectly, and to produce other plastics that were bonded in an impervious coating to the outside surfaces of the rod blanks. Modern solid glass rods do not have the structural weaknesses of the earlier ones. Today's solid glass rods reflect the advances made in technology over a period of more than twenty years, and many manufacturers offer solid glass spinning, fly, and baitcasting rods in their lines. But the solid glass rod in its freshwater versions still carries the reputation that became attached to the first models, and has never gained great acceptance. In saltwater versions, the reverse is the case; solid glass rods are the deserved darlings of deep-sea fishermen, and in this application they are superb.

Continuing experiments with glass filaments embedded in plastics produced rods of an entirely new breed beginning in the late 1940s. These hollow or tubular fiberglass rods are made from a thin mesh or netlike cloth woven of fine glass filaments, wrapped around a tapered mandrel or inner form that is usually made of either balsa wood or steel, and then coated with a plastic resin. The coating material, in which the fiberglass cloth becomes imbedded, is similar to the familiar epoxy glues in that it is activated by a catalyst that causes it to cure by internally generated heat. However, unlike epoxy, which becomes brittle when hard, the resin used in fiberglass rods cures into a very tough, very flexible film that can be controlled as to density and thickness.

After the resin cures, the tapered mandrel is slipped out of the hardened shell, leaving a thin-walled glass and plastic tube. By varying the taper of the mandrel as well as the number of layers of glass mesh and the thickness and density of the resin coating, rod blanks can be produced to give any combination of characteristics in their action. Other variations are possible by altering the pattern of applying the mesh to the mandrel, by changing the diameter of the glass filaments themselves, and by using different types of resins in impregnating the glass fibers. Each manufacturer has a slightly different method of producing tubular fiberglass rods, but the process just described is the basic one by which all such rods are made.

Whether the newest man-made fishing rod material will replace fiberglass is a subject currently being debated by both fishermen and tackle makers. The new material, High Modulus Graphite (HMG) and often simply called "graphite" was introduced in the early 1970s, and is just now undergoing the sort of testing and experimentation to which fiberglass rods were subjected in their beginning days. Invariably, HMG rods are compared to glass rods in terms of action, weight, durability, and so forth, just as in the 1940s and 1950s the new fiberglass rods were being compared to long-familiar rods of split bamboo.

My own experience with HMG rods is limited, but after handling and experimenting a bit with a heavy-duty plug rod and a light fly rod, both made by Fenwick, I'd say that HMG rods come closer than glass to approximating the feel and action of fine bamboo rods. For all its stiffness of action, the plug rod had an incredibly sensitive feel; when using it with a weighted plastic worm in bottom-fishing, I could tell quite easily what type of bottom the lure was working over, and even a light strike was transmitted readily to the rod hand.

Inevitably, I compared the fly rod with my all-time favorite dry-fly rod made by the late E. C. Powell. The chief difference between the two rods was not in their action, but in their weight. The 9-foot Powell rod weighs in at 4⅝ ounces compared to the 2⅞-ounce weight of the 8½-foot Fenwick, although both balance to a #6 line. The Fenwick rod required a slightly faster casting tempo than the Powell, but in sensitivity they are about equal, though my comparisons here were made from memory of the bamboo's sensitivity and with human fingers instead of trout "taking" the fly during my experiments with the Fenwick rod.

HMG rods are both similar to and different from those made of fiberglass. HMG is a synthetic fiber based on the familiar acrylics used in weaving fabrics for clothing. The acrylic material used in rodmaking is first subjected to mild heat, just under 300° Celsius and then converted to carbon by treatment under a more intense heat, 1200°–1500° C. The carbonized fibers are then placed in an oven from which the oxygen is gradually exhausted while the temperature is increased. At 2000°–3000° C., the acrylic fiber alters its structure and is converted to a crystalline graphite. The fibers are then stretched on a steel mandrel, impregnated with a liquid resin, and the coated mandrel is inserted in an outer shell or form while the resin cures.

HMG rods have a much greater strength-to-weight ratio than do rods of tubular fiberglass construction. Their action is, as I've already noted, somewhat stiffer than that of a glass rod in a comparable category. This means that an HMG rod weighing 2 ounces will handle the same weight line, and lay it out as efficiently, as a fiberglass rod weighing 4 ounces; the HMG rod will also be much smaller in diameter and have a more sensitive feel.

The technical term "modulus" as applied to HMG rods is simply a description of the resistance to deflection built into the material of which HMG rods are made. All substances or materials have a characteristic stiffness, and "modulus" means rigidity or resistance to deflection or bending. An HMG rod has approximately three times the modulus of a fiberglass rod molded to be an exact duplicate. In other words, given two rods of identical length, taper, diameter, and wall thickness, one made of fiberglass and the other of treated graphite, the HMG rod would be three times as stiff; if the two rods were bent into the same curve, three times as much weight or energy would be needed to move the HMG rod into the arc.

High modulus in a fishing rod can be both an advantage and a weakness. Low-modulus materials, with a readier acceptance of bending, seldom reach maximum stress in use. Even when playing very heavy fish in big, fast water, a fiberglass rod is seldom worked to more than 35 or 40 percent of its maximum stress. Only when the rod is arced into a complete semicircle does it reach 50 percent of its inherent ability to flex. An HMG rod in the same situation will reach approximately 70 percent of its maximum stress when arced into a quarter-circle. With very little more pressure or bending, then, it reaches the point of 100 percent of maximum stress, and at this point the rod snaps. In this aspect, HMG rods share a characteristic of bamboo rods; perhaps this new material is closing a circle that began in angling's past.

Whatever the material used in their construction, whatever the name of the manufacturer on the rod, all fishing rods in common use today require the same kind of care and maintenance and can be repaired by using the same basic techniques. There are about twenty brands of glass rods that are now distributed and sold nationwide in the United States. These include a number of brands manufactured by firms with which they did not originate, brand names transferred in a corporate purchase or merger, but which in past years had acquired an identity the new proprietors decided to maintain.

Major brands in national distribution include Berkley, Browning/ Silaflex, Daiwa, Fenwick, Garcia/Conlon, Gladding/Harnell, Heddon, Kodiak, Orvis, Scientific Anglers, Shakespeare, St. Croix, True Temper, Wright & McGill/Eagle Claw, and Zebco. In addition to these there are many "house brand" rods made up on blanks manufactured by a firm whose name will generally not appear on the finished rod.

From the standpoint of maintenance and repairs, there is an almost total kinship between fiberglass rods, regardless of who makes them or whether they are spinning, baitcasting, fly, boat, surf, or trolling rods. Their maintenance needs are essentially the same, and the procedures, tools, and materials used in repairing them are virtually identical. All differences as well as similarities will be noted in the sections that follow.

Maintenance Needs Common to All Rods

No matter how carefully you handle your favorite rods, there are times when they'll suffer minor damage during a day of fishing. Usually, this damage is very small indeed, something like a frayed guide wrapping giving way and a guide popping off, a tip-top coming loose, or a reel seat with worn threads slipping and failing to lock the reel in place. Damages such as these can be prevented by regular inspection of your rod, and immediate replacement of the damaged part.

While you're inspecting your rod at the end of the day, it's a good idea to clean it by wiping with a soft cloth, and then to carry the cleaning a step farther by removing the bits of abrasive grit and sand that invariably collect around the guides. The best instrument you'll find for cleaning the guides is a common pipe cleaner. Use it as shown in the picture—one end moistened to pick up the almost invisible debris that accumulates in the crevice between the wrapping at the top

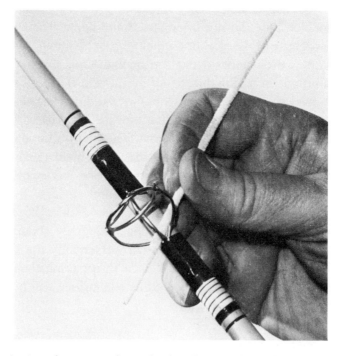

A pipe cleaner is about the handiest tool you'll find when you clean bits of abrasive grit out of the base of a guide.

28

of the feet of the guide and between feet and rod, the dry end as a brush.

Pay special attention to the guides; they're the rod components most often and most easily damaged. This is especially true of the snake guides used on fly rods; it takes only a small bump on a tree or rock to bend one of these out of shape, which may result in a casting impediment or a frayed fly line. Often, a bent snake guide can be straightened with a pair of roundnose pliers. Using carefully controlled pressure on the jaws, start working at the edge of the bend and let the jaw pressure alone restore the guide to its original shape, as shown in the picture. Don't try to make this kind of repair with regular longnose pliers that have flat inner jaws; it can be made successfully only with pliers having full-round jaws. If you don't have a pair, your jeweler

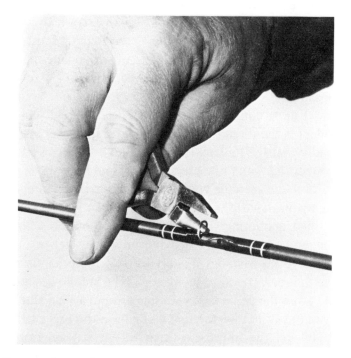

Bent snake guides can sometimes be straightened by applying gentle pressure with roundnose pliers, as shown. Start at one end of the bent spot and move the pliers into the bend a fraction of an inch at a time, pressing each time you move them.

might be persuaded to let you use his, and optometrists also use pliers of this kind.

Ring guides such as those used on casting and spinning rods can seldom be straightened in this fashion, though some spinning rod guides have very thin rings and their metal may be malleable enough to be worked this way. You'll have to try the procedure for yourself on any bent guide you might encounter, since the malleability of the metal used will vary from one brand to another. Heavy ring guides and guides with ceramic or other types of inserted inner rings can't be handled in this fashion, but must be replaced. This job will be covered later in this chapter.

When checking guides, also check their wrappings. A frayed wrapping should be replaced, of course, but this can't always be done at once if you're on a trip far from your home base. Often the wrapping can be mended temporarily by brushing on an extra-heavy coat or two of fly-head cement or clear nail polish, or a coat of varnish. If the fraying is extensive, cover it with a wrap of cellophane tape. This is a purely temporary expedient, and the guide should be rewrapped as soon as possible.

The next most common problem point is the reel seat. Sand and grit can collect in the threads of a reel seat and sooner or later will wear them so badly that the locking ring won't hold tightly. Few things are more disconcerting than to be playing a fish and have the reel come off your rod. For a few seconds you'll stand there with the reel dangling in your hand by its handle, which of course can't be turned because there's nothing anchoring the reel in place. You'll see line slipping through the guides as the fish feels your pressure slacken and takes off on a run, and you'll wish desperately for two more hands so that you can replace the reel. If you're lucky, you'll be able to get the reel back on the rod before the fish winds your line around a snag and breaks off, or you'll run out of line or the line will jam in the reel, with the same result. If you get the impression that this is written from personal experience, you're right. It has happened to me and I've seen it happen to others. Later you may be able to see the humor in this kind of fiasco, but it's not at all funny while it's happening. To prevent it from happening at all, clean your reel seat threads regularly.

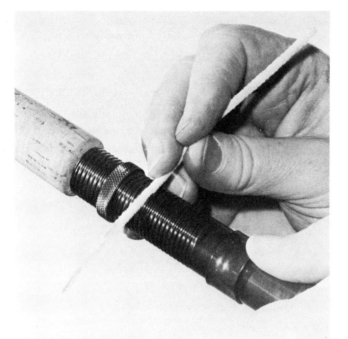

Rotate your rod slowly while pressing a moistened pipe-cleaner into the threads of the reel seat to remove sand and grit that will cut and loosen the threads.

Ferrules also need regular care. Make sure when jointing up a rod that the ferrules are free from grit and show no scratches or rubbed areas that would indicate abnormal wear. All ferrules are designed to mate closely, so they'll show some signs of friction caused by normal jointing and unjointing, but it's very easy to spot potential trouble in the form of deep scratches or badly worn spots. Double the pipe cleaner and swab out the inner walls of the female ferrule, and wipe the male ferrule clean with a soft cloth. Do not at any time put any kind of oil or grease on a ferrule.

We all know that for uncounted decades generation after generation of fishermen have rubbed the male ferrule over their noses to transfer a microscopically thin coating of body oil to its surface. The truth of the matter is that the quantity of oil transferred this way from nose to ferrule is so tiny that it does neither harm nor good. It's a fisherman's tradition—and if it makes you happy to do it, by all means rub.

Nose oil and oil from an oil can are two different things, though. Even the finest oil applied in the stingiest quantity and the ferrule rubbed until it looks and feels oil-free can still bond male and female ferrules together by capillary action. At one time or another, every fisherman has had a frozen ferrule to contend with, and frozen ferrules are no fun. Half the time, or more, injudiciously applied oil is to blame. Just remember that *any* oil is a bad idea where ferrules are concerned.

When you're alone and faced with a rod having frozen ferrules, use the "squat and spread" method to part them. Put the rod behind your knees as shown and with your hands outside your legs grasp the rod. Your hands should be as close to the ferrules as possible.

Having a friend along makes unjointing frozen ferrules easier. Stand facing each other as close together as possible; the fellows in the picture are standing apart to show the position.

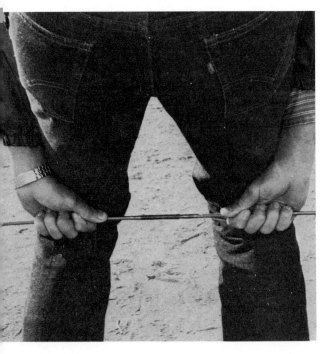

They're made to fit snugly, and those few extra microns by which an invisible oil coating will increase the male ferrule's diameter will often result in freezing.

There are two easy ways to unjoint a frozen ferrule without damaging it. Keep in mind that your objective is to apply a straight-line pull to the ferrule, and that any tool you try to use will bend the ferrule out of shape and perhaps even damage the rod. Nor should you try to free the ferrule by twisting; repeated twists can loosen the adhesive holding ferrule to rod and can permanently damage the end of the rod itself.

If you're alone, hold the rod behind your knees and get a firm grip with one hand on the male, the other on the female ferrule. Now, squat down and spread your knees slowly, pulling your hands apart and, with luck, freeing the frozen ferrule. Don't try to jerk your knees apart, just spread them out slowly until something gives. You may have to do this two or three times, but it usually works.

If you're with someone else, use the four-hand method to unjoint a frozen ferrule. Stand as shown in the photo, facing your companion. You take a firm grip of one ferrule with your right hand, he takes a firm grip of the other ferrule with his right hand. Put your left hand on the rod beyond your friend's right hand while he puts his left hand behind your right hand. Get a firm grip, and both pull at once, firmly and steadily, without jerking. If this doesn't do the job the first time around, give the rod a half-turn and repeat.

If neither method works, you should take the female ferrule off the rod section and gently tap out the male ferrule with a short length of dowel and a hammer. (This will be shown in detail later on.)

Unless you find a trouble spot or a potential trouble spot, you'll spend less than three minutes checking your rod at the end of a day's fishing. Even if you do find a problem, fixing it temporarily will require only another five to ten minutes, and they're minutes well spent. You shouldn't need to do any field repairs more often than a couple of times during a season, but if you fish regularly, chances are that at some time during your fishing days you're going to spot something needing correction that you didn't notice while on the water. A couple of minutes spent checking over your tackle when you come in at the end of the day is the cheapest insurance you've ever bought.

Repairing Glass Rods

There are only two types of damage to a tubular glass rod that the average fisherman, using everyday tools, can't repair himself. Luckily, one of these two types occurs very seldom—this is the kind of extensive crushing, involving from 3 to 6 or more inches of the rod, that occurs when a car door or trunk lid is slammed down on a rod section. A small crushed portion, up to about 2 inches long, can readily be repaired, but a crushed place more extensive than 2 inches calls for replacing the entire section. So does a crushed spot in the upper 12 to 16 inches of a rod tip section, or a tip section broken off cleanly within 12 to 16 inches of the top. If one of your rods suffers either of these damages, bow to the inevitable and replace the section.

All manufacturers of fiberglass rods whose products are distributed nationally maintain a factory stock of replacement rod sections. If the broken rod carries a maker's warranty, and it has not expired, the replacement will cost you nothing except shipping charges. A few makers offer lifetime guarantees on some models of their deluxe rods; this guarantee usually includes a factory registration at the time the rod is bought.

With three exceptions, all U.S. rodmakers require that the entire rod be sent to the factory when one of its sections must be replaced. The exceptions are Berkley, Wright & McGill, and Quick, who advise that certain models of their rods need not be sent in when a replacement section is needed. You will, of course, have to provide such details as the model number and type of rod when ordering the new section. A number of rod manufacturers have authorized service shops or factory-operated repair depots in various parts of the country where rods can be sent or taken to have replacement sections fitted. The dealer from whom you bought the rod can give you details about these if you've lost or thrown away the manufacturer's leaflet that came with the rod.

When you send in a rod for factory repairs, you should at the same time write the Customer Service Department—all manufacturers have one—notifying them of the shipment and giving them details of the repairs needed; similar information regarding repairs should be sent with the rod. Count on at least a couple of weeks between the day you ship and the day your rod will be returned. Figure on an average cost of $5 or $6 for the repair job. If a major replacement is involved, you'll probably be facing a cost of from $8 to $10, or more, unless the rod is still under warranty.

All factory replacements of rod sections are fitted; that is, if you get a new butt section it will have a new grip, reel seat, guides, and ferrules, and its wrappings will match the old tip section. A replacement tip section will have new ferrules, guides, tip-top, and wrapping to match the old butt section. Replacing a section is much less costly than buying a new rod, and doing needed repairs yourself will always cost less than sending in a rod or rod section to a factory or independent repair shop.

Aside from the two major types of damage mentioned earlier, there's no repair job you need to be hesitant about taking on, if you have average digital skill and the few commonplace tools required. Such chores as replacing a guide, resetting a ferrule, even replacing a reel seat and grip, can be done with a minimum of fuss and bother. Splicing a rod that's been crushed in an area of a couple of inches is only a little bit more complicated.

What's true of tubular glass rods is equally true of solid glass rods with one exception—a crushed or broken solid glass rod section cannot be repaired by splicing. If this kind of damage is facing you, a new section is the only answer.

Before getting into details of the jobs themselves, let's dispose of a few generalities and cover such odds and ends as rod and rod fittings nomenclature. To begin with, the bare blank of a fiberglass rod, whether tubular or solid, is frequently called a "blade"—a trade term. A rod or blade might be in one piece, two pieces, or in the case of pack rods, four, five, or even six pieces.

Sections of a rod are joined by ferrules, which may be of metal or integral with the rod. Metal ferrules come in a great variety of styles and are made from several types of metal. Most ferrules used today are made of anodized aluminum, which is relatively soft even when heat-treated, but is much less difficult to form than steel, the next most widely used ferrule material. Steel ferrules are heavily nickel-plated to minimize rusting. By far the best metal for ferrules is nickel silver—formerly called German silver—an alloy of copper, zinc, and nickel, which is rustproof and can be formed to very precise dimensions that the metal will retain for a very long time even under the wear of constant friction as a ferrule is joined and parted. A few European rods are fitted with phosphor bronze ferrules, which has characteristics similar to nickel silver but is appreciably heavier. Better-grade ferrules have solid collars, called welts, while less expensive ones have rolled welts.

Rods having fiberglass ferrules are called self-ferruled rods. There are four types of self-ferruled rods. Fenwick uses a tapered cylinder that mates to the tip of the rod's butt section. Browning uses a similar arrangement, though the taper in the butt section is the normal taper of the rod's butt section. Berkley uses a plug of solid fiberglass inserted in the butt section; tip and butt sections meet over the plug. Heddon molds its rod blanks to allow one section to slip into the other, a variation of the Fenwick and Browning pattern, though there is less apparent enlargement of the female section and less appreciable taper on the male section. All other rodmakers except Scientific Anglers use variations of these patterns; Scientific Anglers uses a twist-on ferrule that is the only one of its kind. By using the plugging repair technique that will be given later on, you can duplicate the Berkley-type ferrule on any of your tubular fiberglass rods if you want to convert them to self-ferruled from metal-ferrule fitted.

There is one other type of ferrule you're likely to encounter—this is the butt ferrule used in attaching a one-piece casting rod blade to its detachable handle. It is shown in the accompanying picture in its component parts as well as its assembled form. The blade is cemented into the top portion of the ferrule, and the ferrule fits into an adjustable collet that is at the top of the separate grip. Some grips require special ferrules, others have universal collets that accept a variety of sizes of butt ferrules.

Now we come to the angler's end of the rod, the butt portion, which is composed of the grip and the reel seat. Reel seats are of two kinds, open-end, used on baitcasting, spinning, and deep-sea rods, where they are mounted between two grips, and closed-end, which are used on fly rods and are mounted below the grip. Reel seats are made from aluminum and steel; rarely will a nickel silver reel seat be encountered on a rod made after about 1960. Some reel seats are made

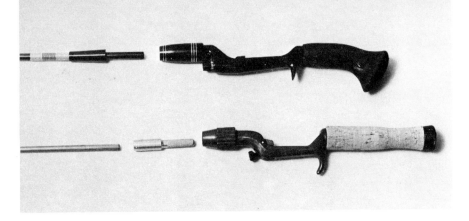

Detachable-grip rods are jointed by fitting the blade with a shouldered ferrule that fits an adjustable collet on the grip. Components for a typical assembly are shown at bottom, an assembled rod at top.

with single locking rings, others have double rings, but this is the only difference in their construction. Light fly rods and spinning rods may have cork reel seats, grooved to accept the foot of the reel, which is secured on the seat by a pair of sliding rings.

Grips—and remember that reels have handles, rods have grips—are traditionally made of cork rings glued together and shaped to whatever contour is desired. As already mentioned, fly-rod grips are located over the reel seat; spinning-rod grips are either one long grip with the reel secured by sliding rings so that it may be placed at the point of best balance, or are divided into rear grip and foregrip with the reel seat fixed between them. On baitcasting rods, the reel seat is always located above the grip, though some rods will have a token foregrip above the reel seat. On heavy-duty rods, such as those designed for deep-sea fishing, the reel seat is generally placed between two full-length grips.

Modern technology has created many substitutes that are appearing on grips in place of the traditional cork. All these substitutes have their own trade names, but basically all of them are made from cork granules or granules of some corklike plastic imbedded in a softer matrix to render the grip slip-resistant. Some of these new materials come in the form of tubing that can be cut to the proper length and slipped over the butt of the rod, others come in molded shapes, still others are molded integrally with the shaft of the grip. The latter type will generally be found on heavy-duty baitcasting rods, and the popular style is in the shape of a pistol butt, which lends these grips their name. In the sequence of accompanying photos, various styles of grips are illustrated and described more fully.

37

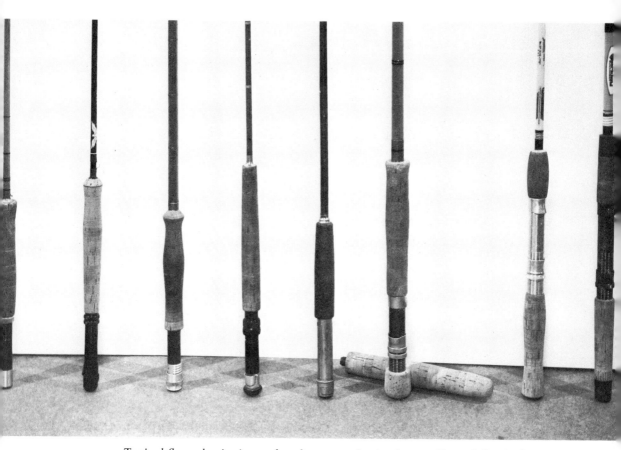

Typical fly and spinning rod reel seats and grip shapes. From left: single-ring metal reel seat, modified Wells cork grip on Winston bamboo fly rod, the modifications are a cupped thumb rest and ringed corks; double-ring, open bottom hood plastic reel seat, half-Wells cork grip on Fenwick HMG fly rod; single-ring top inset hood nickel silver and plastic reel seat, full Wells cork grip on bamboo fly rod by E. C. Powell; button-capped open bottom hood double-ring metal and plastic reel seat, long Payne cork grip on Harisson bamboo fly rod; open bottom hood single sliding ring-plated steel reel seat, short Payne cork grip on very early Granger bamboo fly rod; cork-capped double-hood double-ring anodized aluminum reel seat, enlarged half-Wells grip on fiberglass saltwater fly rod of my own construction, an extension grip that replaces the cork cap lies by the rod; plated brass single-ring reel seat on light Shakespeare fiberglass spinning rod with short cork foregrip and Wells-contour cork bottom grip; plastic single-ring reel seat on medium-weight Berkley fiberglass spinning rod with capped cork full foregrip, grip is Phillippe taper.

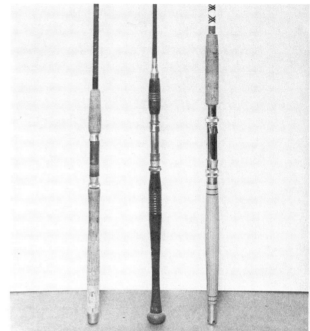

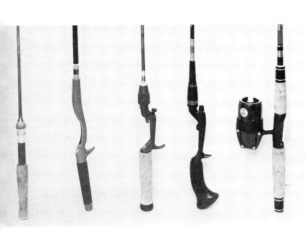

Typical baitcasting reel seats and grips. From left: straight Wells-contoured cork grip, token cork foregrip, inset hood nickel silver and plastic reel seat on ⅝-ounce bamboo tournament rod by E. C. Powell; capped Nextel offset grip, screw-locking Polycarbonate reel seat on Browning STD fiberglass rod; capped cork straight grip, screw-locking Cycolac reel seat by Featherweight, Rawhide fiberglass rod blade; molded offset pistol grip, spring-loaded locking reel seat on Heddon Mark fiberglass rod; cork fore and rear capped straight grip, integral reel on True Temper fiberglass rod.

Typical heavy-duty reel seats and grips. From left: metal-capped full foregrip cork grips, integral hood single-ring metal reel seat on Fenwick tubular fiberglass saltwater rod; rubber-capped full wood grips, integral hood single-ring plated brass reel seat on bamboo light boat rod of my own construction; gimbal-slotted metal-capped wood bottom grip and cork foregrip, integral hood single-ring plated brass reel seat on heavy solid fiberglass rod on Harnell blank by Spinmaster.

Fly rods are fitted with a rigid ring guide called the butt guide or stripping guide, with anywhere from ten to twelve additional snake guides above the butt guide. Spinning rods are fitted with from four to seven ring guides, depending on the length of the rod. These guides are graduated in size either in 64ths of an inch or in millimeters, the measurement being that of the ring's outside diameter. Casting rod guides are also graduated in size and measured in 64ths of an inch outside diameter. The step-down in sizes of the guides from butt to tip is much more pronounced in spinning than in casting rod guides, as the butt guides on spinning rods must serve as funnels to gather the line as it comes looping off the reel and channel it into a straight line to the tip. Guides fitted on deep-sea rods are usually roller guides, the rollers designed to ease line friction. Roller guides are also measured in 64ths of an inch.

Snake guides for fly rods are usually made from stainless or high-tungsten steel; the latter are customarily bronzed. Casting rod guides on older rods are usually of carbon-alloy steel, but the trend is to fit new rods with guides having ceramic or carbide inserts; both these materials take on a smoother, harder finish than does steel. Spinning rod guides with similar inserts are also being more widely used, and many rods are being fitted with antifouling guides that have a long arced foot at their back to reduce line snarls. The picture shows an array of typical guides for various kinds of rods.

Typical guides used on different types of rods. From bottom: Allan ceramic insert butt guide and bronzed snake guide set for fly rods; Varmac ceramic insert guide set for casting rods, packaged in sets as shown; Gudebrod's Aetna foulproof guide set for spinning rods; Fuji Carbaloy guide set for spinning rods; Mildrum roller guides of ocean rods.

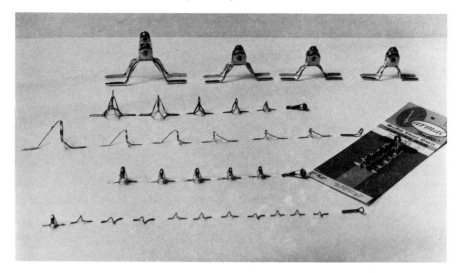

Nylon has emerged as the favored rod-winding thread; you can still find silk if you're trying to match wrappings on an older rod, but you may not be able to find a complete range of colors in silk thread. A few makers used tape as a substitute for thread in setting on guides a few years ago, but the substitution was not really popular or successful, and most of them have now gone back to the traditional thread windings.

One of your biggest problems in replacing a rod component is going to be to match those already fitted to the rod. Knowing exactly what you're looking for is half the battle. From the text and pictures, you should be able to recognize the type of every piece that makes up any fishing rod, and instead of just going out to look for a grip or a guide you can go out looking for a specific kind and size of grip or guide or whatever component you're replacing.

Now, starting with the easiest jobs and going on to the most difficult, let's look at the home-repair jobs you can do on your own fiberglass rods.

Replacing Guides

This is by far the simplest and least complicated of all rod repairs. The only materials needed are a new guide matching the one to be replaced, a short length of masking tape, thread that matches the winding already on the rod, and a few drops each of color preservative and varnish. The only tool needed is one that can be used to trim thread ends. Small, sharply pointed scissors such as manicure scissors are fine; my own favorite tool for trimming rod-winding threads is a pair of cuticle nippers. I find it much easier to use nippers than scissors—the nippers cut closer to the winding with better control and less danger of snipping the winding itself. Avoid trying to use a straight-edged tool such as a razor blade or craft knife unless you are expert in handling them, for any straight-edged cutting tool is apt to slice into the winding no matter how carefully it is used.

If you have an entire set of guides to replace—for instance, if you're taking advantage of a broken or scored guide to modernize an older rod by fitting it with ceramic or carbide-lined guides—it will pay

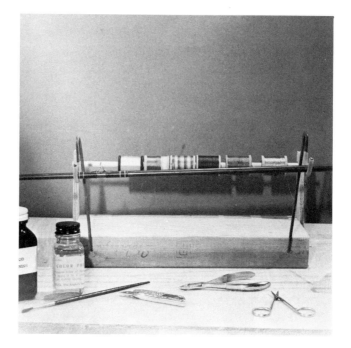

A few minutes' work and some scrap materials produced this holder for use in rod winding. The base is of 2×6 lumber, the arms of heavy clothesline wire forced into slightly undersized holes drilled in the base, the thread support is a length of ⅜-inch dowel held by scraps of 6-inch square plywood nailed to the ends of the base. The only fancy touch is the short length of rubber surgical tubing slipped over the ends of the rod supports to cushion the rods and keep them from shifting and getting scratched while being wound.

you to put together a simple rod holder such as the one pictured. From the photo you can get a clear enough idea of its construction to duplicate it in little more than my total working time of less than fifteen minutes. No dimensions are critical, no tools except a saw, hammer, and drill are needed. The arms that support the rod can just as easily be cut from plywood or hardboard instead of bending them out of clothes-line wire. The only fancy touch I added was slipping a short piece of rubber surgical tubing over the rod supports to keep the metal from scratching the rod being worked on.

There are commercially made rod-winding holders available for around $8, but unless you're going to do a lot of winding, you can make the one illustrated for nothing more than your time, plus pieces of scrap lumber. In his excellent book on rod making (*Fiberglass Rod Making*, Winchester Press, 1974), Dale Clemens gives the plans for a homemade winding holder using furniture casters as a rod support, and if you're going to be doing a lot of winding, you might check it out.

If you have only one or two guides to replace, a holder really isn't necessary. You can simply work freehand, holding the rod in one hand and controlling the thread with a fly-tying bobbin in the other. Or, you can work on a table or desk top or a workbench, passing the winding thread through the pages of a book to maintain tension.

A lot of writers recommend using an armchair in winding rods, but few of them take the trouble to explain that if you use this method you're supposed to sit in the chair with your book and thread on a table or stool in front of you. The first time I ran across this suggestion, many years ago when I first began tackle-tinkering, I reversed the procedure, and sat on a stool in front of the chair with book and thread in the chair seat and the rod resting on its arms. Next to being poised on a slippery rock while playing a big fish in a rushing river, that's the most uncomfortable position I've ever attempted to hold. The picture shows the right way to use an armchair in rod-winding. And, by the way, if you do use a book to maintain thread tension, don't use one that's rare or valuable, but use something disposable, like a telephone directory, for the winding thread is going to cut the book's pages before you're through winding.

Before you can replace a guide, you have to remove the old guide and its wrappings and clean away the remnants of varnish that will cling to the rod when the wrappings are removed. It's wise to unwind the old wrapping thread rather than trying to cut it off, because any blade sharp enough to cut through a couple of coats of tough varnish and color preservative and thread is sharp enough to score the surface

43

This is the right way to organize a setup that uses chair arms to support a rod being wound; you sit in the chair with the thread tensioned by a book on a stool in front of you.

of the rod and perhaps damage it. Instead of slashing away, make one cut at the inside foot of the guide, then unwind the thread by pulling it off the rod. It's quicker to do it this way than it is to try to cut through the wrapping. Just hold the rod loosely and strip away the thread.

Use a piece of crocus cloth to remove the lumps of old color preservative and varnish from the area the windings covered. Never use sandpaper on a rod unless you're cleaning a very badly encrusted spot or reducing the rod's diameter to make a ferrule or tip-top fit correctly. Glass rods are carefully engineered to produce the action they have, and sandpaper cuts into their surface so rapidly that you can quite easily produce a soft spot in the rod before you realize it. Crocus

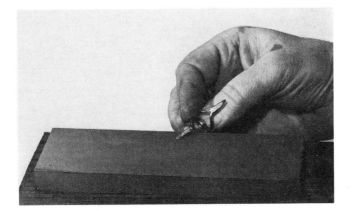

Remove burrs and taper the edges of the guide feet to make wrapping easier by honing the edges thinner, but don't hone the edges into knife-blade sharpness or you risk having them cut the winding thread.

cloth barely cuts; its effect is more one of polishing, and while it means that you'll work a few moments longer when using it, you'll have a better end result. That's what's important.

An alternative to crocus cloth is 4-X steel wool, so fine that it's often called "steel fur." Unlike ordinary commercial grades of steel wool, the 4-X grade polishes rather than cuts, though it does the work faster than the very fine-surfaced crocus cloth. A machinist's supply house or even a first-rate machine shop should have both crocus cloth and 4-X steel wool, if you can't find them at your neighborhood hardware store.

You're now ready to fit the guide on the rod, but your first job is to get the feet of the guide into a condition that will make wrapping them easier. The feet should be flat on the bottom, where usually there's a minute ridge mark left from the forming process, and the edge tapers should be reduced to make it easier for the winding thread to climb over the tips of the feet. Use a simple whetstone for this, working the feet flat, then, as shown in the photo, honing the edges to a fine line— but not one that's so knife-edged it will cut the winding thread. This operation takes only a few moments and makes later work a lot easier.

Positioning the guide is most readily done with a piece of string long enough to reach from the rod's tip-top to its butt. String your guide or guides on the cord, put a dab of masking tape on one foot of each guide you're placing, stretch the string the length of the rod or rod section and you'll be sure that your guides are aligned. When each guide is in its proper place on the rod, press down on the masking tape to hold it, then remove the string before you begin wrapping. There's a good reason for using masking tape. Both cellophane tape and surgical tape leave a residue of adhesive when removed, but masking tape strips away cleanly.

Now comes the wrapping. If you're fitting just one guide, use a thread that matches the wrapping already on the rod, but if you're replacing all the guides, you can use whatever color of thread you fancy. Actually, if you're replacing a guide on an older rod, you might not be able to match the existing wrapping thread, in which case you'll probably want to rewrap all the guides. Gudebrod Bros., the chief source of rod-winding threads, offers sixteen solid colors, twelve two-color combinations, three two-tone color mixtures, one five-color variegated, and six fluorescent colors, which gives you a wide choice. The most useful thread sizes will be D and E, the former for medium to heavy rods, the latter a smaller diameter thread for light rods.

In applying a two-tone wrapping using thread from two different spools, always put on the main wrapping first and add the trim strip later. Before you even begin to wrap, prepare your pull-loop. This is simply a 3- to 4-inch length of thread doubled to form a loop; the ends will need to be twisted a bit so the loop will hold its shape until you're ready to use it in finishing off the wrapping. Put the pull-loop where it will be easy to reach when you need it.

Begin the wrapping about ⅛ inch below the free foot of the guide—the foot not held on the rod by masking tape—as shown in the first photo of the sequence. Start by laying the end of the thread along the rod and wrapping over it with three or four turns, as illustrated; this secures the thread to the rod. True up these first turns by pushing the threads together and aligning them at right angles to the rod. Wrap on four or five more turns, keeping tension as even as possible as you turn the rod. Nylon wrapping thread has a tiny bit of elasticity in it, so it's easy to get the wrap too tight. It should be just firm enough so that

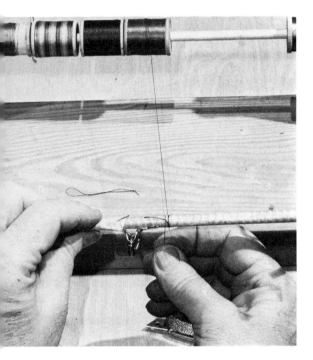 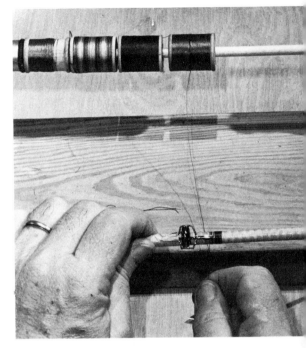

In starting a guide wrapping, hold the end of the thread along the rod and parallel to its length. Take three or four turns over the end as illustrated to anchor it. You can true up these first turns by pushing them with a thumbnail. The loose thread lying along the rod should be trimmed off once you've made ten or twelve turns.

When the wrapping reaches the tip of the guide-foot, make four or five widely spaced turns over the foot, as in the picture, then push them down with your thumbnail until they meet the wrapped portion at right of the guide. This saves the strain of trying to get a single thread to catch on the foot as you start wrapping over it.

passing a fingertip along the wrap with moderate pressure will not move the threads. After you've added a half-dozen turns to your first three or four, trim off the loose dangling end of the thread.

Continue the wrap until you reach the tip of the guide-foot. With a little practice you can feed the thread on at a slight angle so that each turn nestles close to the one that went on before it. When you get to the tip of the guide-foot, without trying to work your tight wrap over the tip, make three or four widely spaced turns, as shown, over the foot. Holding the thread with even tension, push these turns down with your

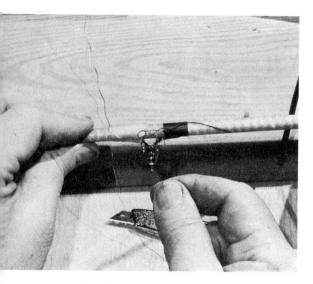

To finish off a wrapping, you must pull the winding thread under itself, that is, under several turns of the wrapping. When your wrapping is within a half-dozen turns of reaching the guide-brace, lay the pull-loop along the rod with its closed end about ½ inch beyond the point where the wrap will end. Then wrap over the pull-loop until you have put on those final few turns.

Cut the wrapping thread, leaving about 1 inch to be pulled under. Pass the end of the wrapping thread through the loop, grasp the other end of the loop threads—both of them—and pull with one smooth unhurried tug.

thumbnail until they cover the tip of the guide-foot and nestle against the thread already on the rod.

Carry the wrapping up the foot of the guide until you can see that only a half-dozen turns will bring the thread to the base of the ring-brace. Now, put the pull-loop in place as shown, under the wrapping thread, with the closed end sticking out beyond the portion that will be covered when the wrap is completed. Finish winding, going over the loop, until the ring-brace is reached. Cut the wrapping thread, leaving about 1 inch of excess length. Slip the end of the wrapping thread through the loop, grasp both ends of the loop threads that stick out between the wrapping, and pull the loose end of the wrapping thread under the wrap. Discard the loop and trim the protruding loose end of the wrapping thread off flush with the wrap.

There will probably be some small gaps or irregularities in your wrapping at this point. Press with both thumbnails against opposite ends of the wrap; this should push the threads together tightly as well as truing up both ends of the wrapping at right angles to the rod. It may be necessary to rub your thumbnail lightly over any large gaps to close them up. Over the years, I've tried a number of tools on this job of making the final adjustment of rod wrappings, but until recently had not found anything that would equal a thumbnail for the job. The back of a table knife, a toothpick, various kinds of rubber erasers, all fuzzed up and marked the wrapping thread when used with enough pressure to be effective. Then, recently, it occurred to me that a new kind of typewriter eraser might be effective. Actually, it's not really an eraser, but is a pliable plastic cylinder in a pencil-type casing that lifts marks off paper. I have tried it on both nylon and silk windings and it works perfectly, leaving no marks on the thread even when rubbed back and forth along the winding with considerable pressure. If you want to try it, get an A. W. Faber #1966 Rub-Stick, and use it with a fairly blunt tip.

If you want a two-tone wrapping, now's the time to add a trim wrap at each end of the wrapping that secures the guide, using a different color thread. It goes on just as did the longer wrapping. Turn the rod end for end and remove the masking tape, then wrap the second foot in place just as you did the first. When both feet have been wrapped, apply at least three coats of color preservative; this will keep the thread from changing color when varnished. After the color preservative is dry, varnish the wrapping, using two or three thin coats. The last step is to pick up a scanty drop of varnish on the end of a toothpick or splinter of wood and work it in around the inside of the guide to seal the triangle left between the wrapping and the rod at the end of the wrap, where the guide-foot is thickest.

Let the rod rest horizontally and turn it occasionally during the first half-hour or so after the varnish has been applied. If hung up vertically at once the varnish coat is apt to sag, especially in warm weather. All varnishes will do this at times. The varnish you've used should match that already on the other wrappings; most rods are finished with spar varnish, which you can buy in 1- or 2-ounce bottles at tackle shops. Newer rods may be finished with an epoxy, and this, too, is sold in tiny bottles by tackle dealers.

Well-stocked tackle stores will also have assortments of guides, but you may not be able to match the guides on old rods. Most guidemakers package guides in sets, and these are more commonly stocked than are loose guides. If you have a problem finding guides to match those on old rods, you can either put on an entire new set, or try to find matching guides from one of the supply sources listed in the Appendix.

Replacing Rod Tip-tops

Top guides on all rods are called tip-tops to distinguish them from the rod tip itself. When a tip-top is broken off, a bit of the rod goes with it 99 percent of the time. This usually has little effect on a rod's action, unless the break is on an ultralight fly or spinning rod, in which case it's a good idea to slip on a new tip-top and hold it in place with masking tape long enough to check out the action and determine whether you'll be satisfied just replacing the tip-top, or whether you'll want to replace the entire rod section. If you decide on the latter course, don't throw away the old section, but fit it with a new tip-top and keep it as a spare against some day of dire emergency.

Most fly rods are fitted with free-loop tip-tops, which have no braces running from loop to the barrel. Braced or reinforced tip-tops are customarily used on spinning and baitcasting rods, but you may find them on some heavy-duty fly rods. Deep-sea rods are fitted with roller tips that match their guides. All tip-tops are measured in 64ths of an inch, the measurement being that of the inside barrel diameter. Generally when a broken tip-top is replaced, you'll need one of a slightly larger size than that originally fitted to the rod.

To replace a tip-top, you'll need the tip-top guide plus the same tools used in replacing a guide. You'll also need ferrule cement or epoxy glue. Most rodmakers now set their tip-tops and ferrules with epoxy, but I prefer a liquid ferrule cement that will reliquify when heated. Rod fittings set with epoxy must be filed off. Pliobond makes a

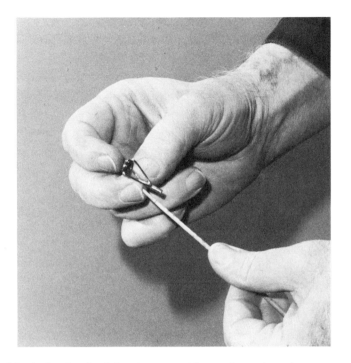

Mark the depth of the tip-top guide on the rod to give you a line to work to; holding the guide beside the tip gives you a preliminary mark that will be refined later.

very satisfactory rod cement and is available at most auto supply stores, hardware stores, and gasoline stations.

The first step in setting a replacement tip-top is preparing the rod top. If the break is jagged, trim it evenly with a fine-tooth saw; a hacksaw will do the job well, but a razor saw such as those found in hobby shops is better. The Exacto people make razor-saw blades that fit the handles of Exacto tools, and most hardware and hobby shops stock them. After doing any required trimming, smooth the rod tip with a bit of crocus cloth. Hold the tip-top up beside the rod tip so that the tip of the rod is even with the point at which the tip-top's barrel constricts, and mark the rod tip at the base of the tip-top's barrel.

Your objective is a very tight fit between rod tip and tip-top, so the tip-top you select should be a hairsbreadth smaller in its inner diameter than the outside diameter of the rod tip. Reduce the rod tip's diameter with the very finest grade—#440—of wet or dry sandpaper, which any auto body shop or auto supply store has in stock. Work by rolling the rod tip between a piece of folded sandpaper. Don't try to take off all the excess material at one time, reduce the rod's diameter a bit, try it in the tip-top for size, and keep reducing and trying until you have a smooth, snug fit. To keep track of your progress, when the tip-top can be slipped on the rod for the first time, mark the point where its base reaches and use the two marks now on the tip as your references in doing additional sanding.

Measure your progress by slipping the tip-top on the rod and marking the point reached by the bottom of its barrel.

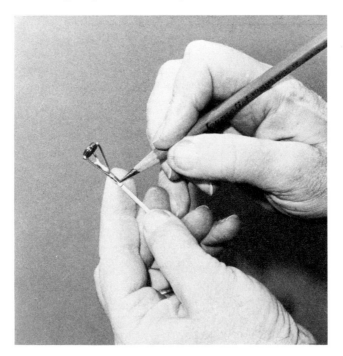

When you have achieved a perfect fit between rod tip and tip-top, spread a thin coating of adhesive on the rod tip. Then put a drop of adhesive on a toothpick and work it inside the barrel of the tip-top, as shown, to get a thin bubble-free coating on the inner wall of the tip-top barrel. If you put too much adhesive in the tip-top, it will not slide all the way down on the rod tip and the excess adhesive will collect in the top of the guide's barrel. Slip the tip-top on the rod tip, being sure it's

Use a toothpick to coat the inside of the guide's barrel and to break up bubbles the adhesive forms. An air bubble in the guide will cause it to creep slowly up after you've put it in place; if this happens, remove the guide and remove some adhesive from the inside with a clean toothpick and push it into place again.

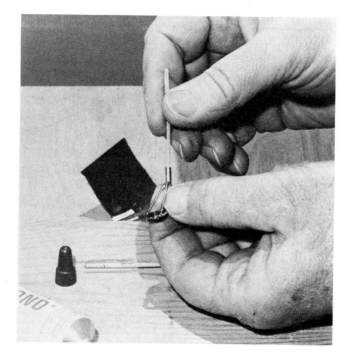

aligned properly with the guides. If necessary, use a piece of string to get perfect alignment.

After the tip-top is placed on the rod, while the adhesive is still soft, use a toothpick to taper the excess adhesive up the rod tip to make it easier for you to carry the wrapping thread over the bottom of the tip-top's barrel. Then, when the adhesive has dried, wrap the joint as previously shown. I like to carry a tip wrapping from about ¼ inch below the tip-top's barrel up over the barrel for another ⅛ inch or so. Since the tip of a rod is so small and delicate, it's not practical to remove any material from the rod itself, and tapering the bottom of a tip-top's barrel on a whetstone is a tedious job. By fairing the joint with the excess adhesive, a very smooth wrapping becomes easy.

Setting Ferrules

Metal ferrules are easy to handle, but if you have a self-ferruled rod you will probably be well advised to send the rod in for factory repair or replacement. In some cases, the ferrules on self-ferruled rods cannot be successfully replaced, and a new section must be fitted.

While the job of replacing a plug-type glass ferrule isn't beyond the skill of an amateur tackle craftsman, it does have one tricky process. This is removing the broken piece of plug that's probably stuck in the female joint and reaming out the piece that's in the male joint. Unless this process is handled very carefully, removing the broken section of plug from the male joint may weaken the rod's walls. If you want to try your hand at it, knowing the problem in advance, the details will be covered later in this chapter.

Fenwick and Browning, both of which use a tapered male section that mates into a similarly tapered female ferrule, advise against anything but factory work on their rods. The tapers involved are very precise and require the use of factory equipment to get a well-fitted joint. Metal ferrules, however, can be replaced quite easily when bent or broken, or when you simply want to upgrade an inexpensive rod by putting on high-quality ferrules. When replacing metal ferrules, always put on both the male and female pieces to ensure getting a satisfactory fit. First take off any wrappings and then remove both male and female ferrules. If the ferrules have been set with a liquid adhesive or with thermosetting ferrule cement, this simply means heating the ferrule until the old adhesive starts to bubble out around its rim.

Often the heat from a wooden kitchen match is enough to do the heating job, but it's easier to handle if you have a stationary heat source. A candle is fine, but sooty; an alcohol or butane burner, such as the one shown in the picture, gives clean, soot-free heat and is very satisfactory. Turn the ferrule while holding it about an inch above the heat source, and have a piece of cloth ready to hold it with when you slip it off, to protect your hand. Wipe the rod end clean at once, while the adhesive is still soft; it will save time later on.

If the ferrule you're replacing has been broken off, you can probably tell by inspection what type of adhesive was used to set it. Thermosetting stick ferrule cement will show as a dark brown or black line between rod and ferrule; thermosensitive rubber-based liquid cements, which also soften when heated, will be yellow to orange in color; epoxy will show as a white or translucent line. If you can't tell by looking what kind of adhesive was used, try heat first. If this doesn't soften the adhesive, it has been set with epoxy.

Remember that both male and female ferrules must be replaced. All the procedures given in removing, testing, and setting ferrules must be carried out twice, once in setting the female, once in setting the male.

Filing off an epoxy-set ferrule must be done with care to avoid damaging the end of the rod. Protect the rod by wrapping it well with cloth and place it in a vise; tighten the jaws only enough to hold the rod firmly. The rod wrappings won't need to be removed, they'll come off during the filing. Start with a coarse file and work in a line from one end of the ferrule to the other. When you see that you're breaking through the ferrule wall, switch to a smooth-cut file and continue until you have opened a thin white glue line the entire length of the ferrule.

Start breaking the ferrule from the rod with a pair of wire-cutting pliers, often called "diagonals" or "dikes." Put the tip of one jaw in the exposed glue line at a slight downward angle so that when you begin to apply pressure the tip will be forced in between the ferrule and the rod. Put pressure on gently. When you've forced the tip of the plier jaw under the seam just a tiny bit, move the pliers a fraction of an inch

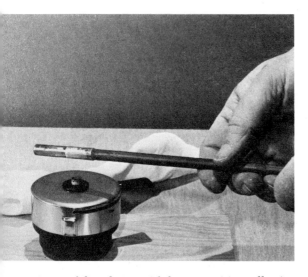

A metal ferrule set with heat-sensitive adhesive needs to be heated only a minute—quite literally, 60 seconds—to soften the adhesive. A butane burner such as the one shown in the photo is handy when you're setting ferrules or reel seats.

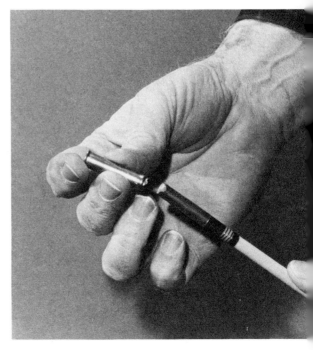

Most common point of ferrule breakage is in the female ferrule at its shoulder.

and take another tiny bite, then move them again and still again, gently forcing just the tip of the jaw into the crack, until you can lay most of the upper jaw into the opened gap.

Now you can take a pretty healthy bite. Hold the upper jaw of the pliers firmly in the crack, set the lower jaw about a third of the way around the ferrule, and close the pliers gently while twisting them away from the crack to force the thin metal along its inner edge out of contact with the glue. You'll hear a slight crack as the glue bond breaks loose, and you can then use a pair of long-nose pliers to pull the ferrule free, as the illustration shows. You probably won't be able to remove the ferrule with your fingers, and if you try to there's a risk of getting a pretty bad cut from the sharp edges created by filing and bending.

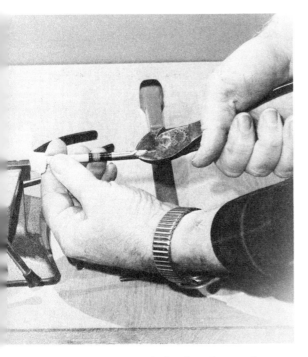

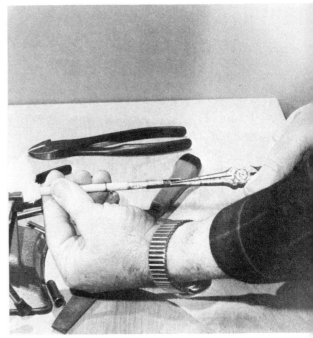

Break into the opened glue line by gentle pressure with the tips of wire-cutting pliers as detailed in the text. When you've created a gap wide enough to allow insertion of the edge of the pliers, use them in an outward and upward twisting motion to break the glue bond.

Don't cut your fingers trying to slide the ferrule off; friction between it and the glue will make it a bit tight. Use long-nose pliers as illustrated to remove the ferrule with a straight pull.

Remove the glue from the end of the rod; start with #440 wet or dry sandpaper and switch to crocus cloth after you've gotten most of the glue layer off. When you're down to the surface of the rod, check the end for roundness and flatness. If you own or can borrow a vernier caliper, the job is easier, but a wrench with flat, parallel, adjustable jaws can be used instead, as pictured.

Try the new ferrule for size; if it refuses to go on, reduce the outer diameter of the rod end. If it goes on but sticks before it is on

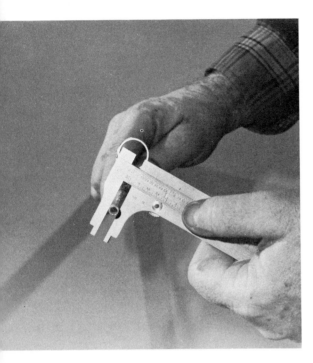

Vernier calipers are the ideal measuring instrument for rod work. With the jaws set, rotate the end of the rod as illustrated while moving it back and forth to discover any areas that are out of round.

Use the calipers this way to test the end of the rod for parallel and to determine the ferrule size needed.

completely, you've got a high spot. If it goes on easily but wobbles as it is turned, you've got a low spot. To find such spots, rub the end of the rod with a soft pencil or powdered carpenter's chalk, slip on the ferrule and turn it a few times. When it's removed, high spots will be rubbed free, low spots will still be covered with graphite from the pencil or with chalk. High spots can be reduced with crocus cloth, but low spots must be built up.

To build up a low spot, tear tissue paper into strips, put epoxy on the low spot, lay a strip of tissue paper in the glue and smooth it with a bit more glue applied on top of the paper strip. Smooth on as many layers of tissue paper as required to remove the low spot, applying thin

A wrench such as the crescent shown in the picture makes a good substitute for vernier calipers. Use it just as you would the calipers to test for roundness and parallel in the outer wall, and find the ferrule size by measuring the gap between the inside of the jaws.

coats of epoxy between each strip. Remove excess paper by sanding after the glue dries. Out-of-round rod ends and undersized rod ends created by too much sanding can be built up this way as well. Your objective in setting a ferrule is not to fit it to the rod end so closely that it must be driven into place, but to fit it just closely enough to leave a hairsbreadth of space between the rod and the ferrule, which the glue will fill. When you've fitted the first ferrule, don't glue it, but fit the mating ferrule on the other rod end. The procedure is the same as that followed in fitting the first one.

After both ferrules have been dry fitted, wrap a wide-spaced spiral of winding thread around each of the rod ends and put the ferrules on. You should have to use some force to push them into place. Joint up the rod and roll it across a tabletop or other flat surface that will allow the grip to hang over the edge to test the rod for straightness. If it isn't straight, you've got some more building up to do with epoxy and tissue paper, or some high spots to reduce, in one or both ferrules. Use the methods already given to cure any misfit you might discover. Each job of setting ferrules is an individual one, and there are no rules I can give you to go by. You'll just have to work by trial and error, but all the techniques you will use have been described.

Finally, when you're satisfied that the ferrules are truly aligned, put a thin coat of epoxy on the rod ends and slip the ferrules in place. Let the glue dry thoroughly before jointing the rod. Then, wrap it to match the other wrappings; the method is the same as that given for wrapping guides.

Replacing Reel Seats

As already noted, there are two types of reel seats, the closed seats used on fly rods and the open-end seats used on spinning and baitcasting rods. There's very little work involved in replacing a fly rod reel seat, since the grip doesn't have to be disturbed. If it's an open-end reel seat on a spinning or bait rod that must be replaced, however, either the foregrip and guides must be removed, or the bottom grip must be cut off. This involves replacing a grip, and isn't all that tough a job unless you make the grip itself, which can become a bit time-consuming.

The basic procedures are the same for putting on a reel seat on any kind of rod. Fly rod reel seats are standardized to 40/64ths of an inch internal diameter. They are not mounted directly on the rod, but on cork or wooden plugs or spacers that are first fitted to the rod blade with adhesive. Usually a thermosetting stick ferrule cement or a liquid ferrule cement is used in fitting reel seats, since epoxy does not adhere satisfactorily to such porous materials as wood and cork.

Your first job, of course, is removing the old reel seat. It may be a modern reel seat that has stripped or badly worn threads, or an old-style slide-lock reel seat, which is going to be replaced with a modern screw-lock type. Remove the reel seat by heating it, the same procedure used in taking off a ferrule set with heat-sensitive adhesive.

Usually, the spacers will need no work, but if it's an old rod, made before the inner diameters of reel seats were standardized, some attention is going to be necessary. Measure the new reel seat against the spacers and saw off the spacer section if it's too long. Then, with a coarse file, reduce the spacers to the required diameter. As in fitting ferrules, your objective is a good, snug fit. You can skip sanding, since you'll get a better bond if the wood or cork surface is a bit rough.

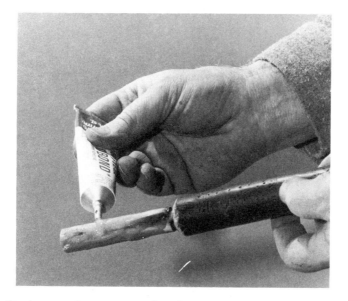

Reel seat plugs are made of porous materials, cork or wood, which will absorb a certain amount of glue, so apply adhesive generously.

Apply adhesive, as illustrated, then slide the new reel seat into place. Be sure you get the seat placed so that the fixed reel-retaining hood is aligned with the guides.

Removing a rod grip on a spinning or baitcasting rod usually means cutting off a cork grip and installing a new grip to take its place after the reel seat has been fitted. If the rod being worked on has a very short foregrip, it may be easier to cut this away and take the reel seat off from the top, even if this requires taking off the butt guides in order to slide the old seat off, the new one on, and then to slip on the new grip. However, if the rod has a foregrip almost as long as the bottom grip, as do many spinning rods, then the bottom grip will probably be a better choice for removal. Whichever grip is removed can be replaced with a preformed grip or with one you form yourself, following the procedures given later in this chapter.

Should the reel seat have been set using epoxy, it must be filed off, using the same technique as for filing off an epoxy-set ferrule. The filing job won't be as difficult in this case, as you'll have no worry about the possibility of damaging the rod if you file too deeply.

Reel seats for spinning and baitcasting rods come in 46/64ths, 52/64ths, and 60/64ths inside diameters, so when selecting a replacement reel seat be sure to get one having the proper inside diameter to fit the spacers already on the rod, or it will be necessary to install new spacers as well as a new seat. The installation is exactly like that of setting a reel seat on a fly rod.

Heavy rods used for deep-sea fishing have detachable bottom grips, which are fitted with a reel seat machined to accept a male ferrule fitted to the butt of the rod. Seats for these big rods come in ¾ inch and ⅞ inch inside diameters, so be sure your replacement seat is the correct size. The seats on deep-sea rods are usually fitted on the lower grip, and are frequently fitted not only with adhesive, but have pins, brads, or screws that attach them to the grip. These must be removed before the old seat can be taken off. The reel seat and male ferrule that go on the rod butt are customarily sold as a unit, and both seat and butt ferrule should be replaced to be sure you'll have a good join. The procedure is the same as that used in setting a fly rod reel seat; the only difference is the size of the fittings involved.

Replacing Rod Grips

While many rod manufacturers are using material other than cork in rod grips, this thick, lightweight tree bark continues to be the first choice for grips, just as it has been for many years. Most attempts to switch away from cork in grips are being made because cork is increasingly short in supply and virtually all of the world's cork comes from countries where political and economic uncertainties have prevailed for a number of years.

Most of the substitute grip materials use cork granules or corklike plastic granules embedded in a porous plastic base. The grips themselves are formed by injection-molding, which requires that they be fitted on a standardized base. This is easily done where new rods are concerned, but it's hard to see how such preformed bases could be applied to the millions of rods now in use, few of which conform to any kind of universal standard in their butts.

Unless you're replacing the grip on a detachable-butt type of rod, you'll be using cork, either in the rings from which grips are formed from scratch, or as one of the several kinds of preformed cork grips. These preformed grips are readily available in a wide variety of sizes and styles. Together with the cork spacers used between rod and reel seat and the cork rings, you can form just about any type of grip you want. These rings are also used to repair grips on the rod, as will be shown later on.

To build a cork grip from scratch, you will need fourteen or fifteen rings for a fly rod grip, twelve to fourteen for a rear grip on a baitcasting rod, four to six rings for the foregrip on a baitcasting rod, twenty-six to thirty rings for a long one-piece spinning rod grip, or sixteen to eighteen for the rear grip and six to eight for the foregrip of a spinning rod with a fixed center reel seat. Cork rings come in $1\frac{1}{8}$-inch and $1\frac{1}{2}$-inch outside diameters and with inside diameters of $\frac{1}{4}$, $\frac{5}{16}$, $\frac{3}{8}$, $\frac{7}{16}$, $\frac{1}{2}$, and $\frac{5}{8}$ inch. To make a typical fly rod grip, your needs would be governed by the taper of your rod from the top to the bottom of the area where the grip would be fitted, graduating the inside diameter of the rings to match the rod's taper and their outside diameter to match the formation the grip would follow. In making a grip for any kind of rod, the number of rings and the inside and outside diameters of each two or three rings would be governed by the outside diameter of the rod butt and the curves the grip will follow in its outside contours.

If you're like most fishermen and have a pet rod with a grip that fits your hand, there's an easy way to duplicate that grip for your other rods. As shown in the first of the accompanying two pictures, take a length of soft wire—coreless solder or a strand of aluminum wire used in big electric transmission cables is ideal—and mold it along the contours of your favorite grip. Then lay the bent wire on a piece of cardboard, trace the contour, and cut along the line you've traced. The result will be a template that you can follow in the shaping of a new grip. (Use of the template will be shown in a later picture.) If you want to build a grip that conforms to any of the traditional patterns, then use the contours in the sketch that follows the pictures. To make a working

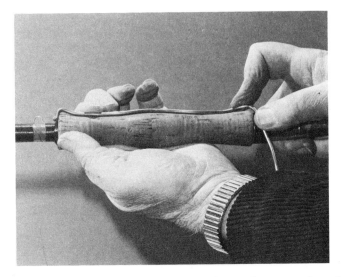

To duplicate a favorite grip on another rod, press a length of pliable wire in a straight line along the grip's contours. Coreless solder is very satisfactory for this purpose.

Lay the formed wire on a piece of cardboard and trace off its outline, then cut along the mark to make a template.

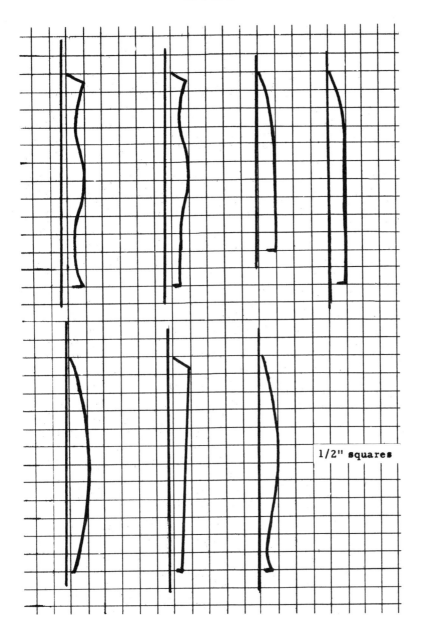

Traditional fly rod grips can be duplicated by making templates from the profiles in this sketch. From top left, these traditional shapes are: Wells, half-Wells, short Payne, long Payne; from bottom left: Phillippe cigar, Phillippe taper, Hardy.

template from the sketches, mark off a piece of cardboard into ½-inch squares and transfer the pattern of the contour you wish to use, cut along the contour lines, and use it as a guide in forming the grip.

To form a cork grip from scratch, you will need in addition to the rings a length of screw-threaded stock ¼ inch in diameter, washers and nuts for each end, wrenches with which to tighten the nuts, and waterproof glue. You can use Pliobond if you wish, but I've had such good luck with resin-based glue that this kind would be my first choice. It's easy to mix, sets up fast, and though it's messy to work with in gripmaking, it does an excellent, permanent job.

As shown in the picture, a large locking wrench is useful to hold the threaded bolt stock, but a vise or even a couple of blocks of wood between carpenter's clamps work equally well. Your first step is to spin a nut on the threaded stock and carry it up about 2 inches from the end, then drop a couple of washers on it. Put on the first cork ring, smear its upper surface with glue, then add rings of the proper inner and outer diameters—which you've worked out in advance by trying the rings on the rod butt for fit—after smearing both faces of each ring with glue. When you come to the last cork ring, apply glue only on its bottom face.

Now, use a piece of waxed paper or plastic wrap to keep the glue off your hands while moving the rings into rough alignment. When you've got the rings fairly straight in relation to each other, put on the top washers and lock nut and tighten it until the rings are firmly compressed. Realign any rings that may have slipped. You'll have to do this a couple of times while you tighten down on the top bolt very firmly indeed—so firmly that most of the glue will ooze out of the spaces between the rings. When this step is completed, find something else to do while the glue dries; depending on temperature and humidity, this will take from two to four hours, perhaps even longer. Be patient, though, and don't try to proceed until the glue is completely dry.

If you have a lathe or a vertical drill press, or access to either, the shaping job can be done with a bit more ease than if you have to improvise a way to hold an electric drill in a fixed position while it spins the glued-up corks. In the picture, I've used a vise to hold the auxiliary handle of my drill, but a stand that holds such a drill horizontally or

In building a cork grip from scratch, a piece of threaded bolt stock is used as a press. Put the threaded stock upright in a vise or use a heavy wrench with locking jaws as in the picture to hold the bolt stock while the rings are assembled. A nut topped with washers is threaded on the bottom end of the bolt stock before the assembly begins.

vertically would do the same job. If you work with the glued-up corks horizontal, then you'll need a block of wood to put under the end of the threaded stock so the drill won't sag when you begin filing and sanding.

Your tool and material needs at this point, in addition to the drill, are a couple of files and at least three grades of sandpaper from coarse to very fine. I usually begin with a #36 garnet cabinet paper, go from it to #80 paper of the same type, and finish the first shaping with #120 paper. The files I use are a half-round mill bastard to begin with, which

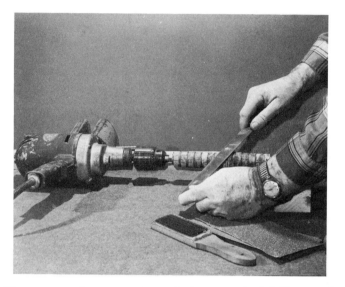

If you own or have access to a lathe or vertical drill press, it will be somewhat easier to form the grip, but an electric hand drill will do the job just as fast and as efficiently. You will need to have a method of holding the drill. In my lashup in the picture, the auxiliary top handle of the drill is held in the vise just behind it and a block of wood supports the end of the bolt stock not chucked in the drill. Keep a file card handy and clean your file often while you work.

is fast-cutting and very handy in forming curves; then I go to an 0-cut smooth file before switching to sandpaper.

Do the first rough shaping by filing freehand against the direction of the drill's rotation to bring the cork rings, now a cylinder, to approximate contours. When the grip begins to take shape—and it doesn't take long, for cork cuts easily, so easily that you'd best work slowly until you get the feel of it—then switch to the smooth file and begin to look occasionally at your template. When the roughness of the original shaping has been reduced by the smooth file, switch to sandpaper of the coarsest grade. Now it's time to begin stopping the drill

Use the template by stopping the drill occasionally and pushing the contoured edge of the template against the cork cylinder while turning the drill slowly with one hand.

When about ⅛ inch more cork needs to be removed to bring the grip to its final shape, switch to fine sandpaper and use the template frequently. If you find it helps to mark areas needing attention, by all means do so; the pencil marks will be removed in the finish sanding.

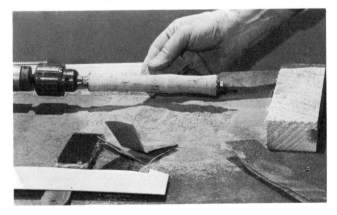

occasionally and turning it by hand while you hold the template against the grip, as illustrated. This will show you exactly where to use more pressure, where to use less, in applying the sandpaper to the grip.

Wind up the preliminary shaping with the finest grade of sandpaper, and use the template often. By now, the grip should be in its final form, needing only a few finishing touches. The first finishing touch is to take the grip out of the drill and out of its holding shaft, and round off the ends with very fine sandpaper. Then, with a rattail file, true up the center hole. Inevitably, there'll be a small amount of misalignment, and this must be cured by filing. Work from both ends of the grip, using the file with a very light touch, and remove as little material as possible from the center hole.

Your final step is to put the grip back on the shaft and chuck it in the drill once more while you polish it with #440 wet or dry paper used wet. Remember, this time you're just polishing, so use a strip of paper and the smallest possible amount of pressure on the grip. The finished grip should look like the one in the final picture, smooth and without any wide and obvious glue lines.

Making a rod grip from scratch is another of those jobs that looks complicated and seems complicated when you're reading about it, but is really quite easy and straightforward and doesn't take all that much time. Excluding the time spent waiting for glue to dry, your total working time in making your first grip should be less than forty-five minutes, and half that for the next ones you make.

Fitting the finished grip to the rod is merely a matter of coating the bare, cleaned rod blade with adhesive, either phenolic resin waterproof glue of the kind used in gluing up the grip, or Pliobond, and sliding the grip into place.

There will probably be times when you'll be working on a rod that tapers to a diameter smaller than that of the smallest inner diameter rings, or you will be a bit too ambitious in using the rattail file on the center hole and will wind up with a center hole bigger than the diameter of your rod. Don't worry—this can be cured. Basically, it's the same problem you'll encounter when fitting almost any preformed grip, since their inner holes always seem to be bigger in diameter than that of the rod to which you want to fit them.

Here's how your finished grip will look. If the cork used is very porous, it can be rubbed with a wood filler and repolished.

When you run into this problem of an oversized center hole in a grip, reach for a ball of heavy twine or cord. Wrap a smooth layer up the butt of the rod as far as the grip will go, as shown in the photo. Check the grip hole for size, and if it's still too big, overwrap in the opposite direction. You can correct the taper of any rod to almost any size center hole in a grip by winding the rod butt until you've formed a cylindrical wrap of twine. Soak the twine well with adhesive. (A liquid adhesive such as Pliobond is a good choice.) Then, push the grip into place, and you'll have a nicely fitted, tight grip.

Not all damaged grips must be replaced with an entire new grip. In cases where only two or three rings of a cork grip have been severely damaged, it's quite practical to insert two or three new corks to replace those that have been chewed up.

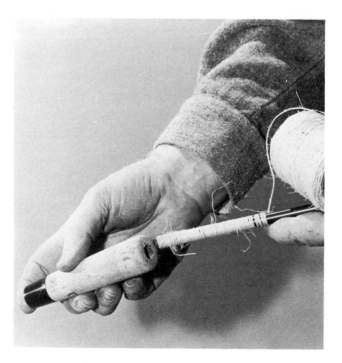

Any grip, preformed such as this one or one you've made yourself, can be fitted to a rod with a diameter smaller than the grip's center hole. Wrap the rod butt evenly with twine to bring the butt up to the desired diameter.

The first step is to remove the damaged corks, for which you'll need a razor-sharp knife, preferably one with replaceable blades, because cork is a material that sands and files easily but is very tough to cut. Make your first cut into one of the damaged corks just below the glue line of the sound cork that will remain on the grip. Your first cut should be a shallow one, carried around the grip, keeping the knife blade about ⅛ inch under the glue line that separates the damaged cork from the sound one. Deepen the cut with successive passes until you can feel the surface of the rod touching the knife.

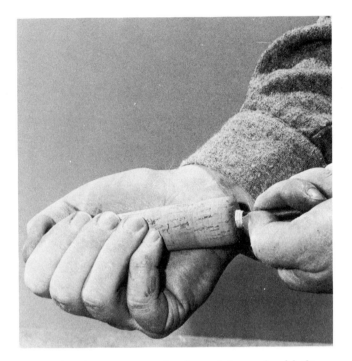

A grip fitted over a cord-enlarged butt should fit very snugly. A healthy push should be required to seat it after the adhesive has been applied. If a few turns of the cord stick up above the grip, trim them off after the glue dries; the grip check will hide them on the finished rod.

Now, make a deep cut at the opposite end of the damaged area. Don't cut right at the glue line, but keep about ⅛ inch away from it. Go around the grip, removing as much of the damaged cork as is possible without cutting into the rod itself. The reason for cutting away from the glue line is that cork crumbles when cut, and you want those new cork rings you're going to insert to fit tightly against the ones left on the grip. After you've removed most of the old, damaged rings, make careful shallow cuts right on the glue line at both ends, shaving away the remaining bits and chunks of old cork.

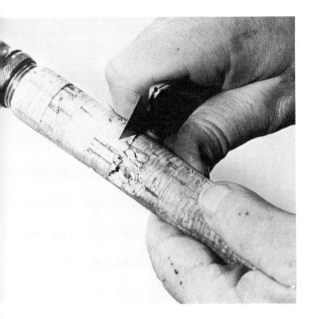

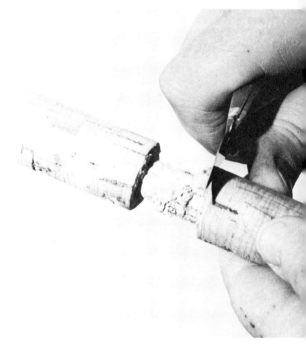

Cut straight down on the cork that's to be removed; make the cut about ⅛ inch from the ring that will be left on the rod. Use the glue line to guide your cut and have your knife razor-sharp. Make a shallow scoring cut, then deepen it with repeated passes until you feel the knife touch the rod.

When most of the old cork has been removed, cut straight down at the glue line at both ends of the opened area. Make shallow cuts, shaving rather than cutting away big chunks of cork.

Level the faces of the exposed cork rings on the rod with a file. If you have a warding file—a file with one toothless or "safe" face—use it, keeping the safe face in contact with the rod. Lacking such a file, use a strip of fine sandpaper stretched along a block of scrap lumber, with no sandpaper on the side of the block in contact with the rod. What you're doing here is creating a 90-degree angle between the rod and the cork rings remaining on it so that the new rings will fit tightly.

Select two new cork rings. Don't worry about their width, all these rings are exactly ½ inch thick. With a rattail file, enlarge their center holes until the holes are the same diameter as the rod section they will go around. If you wait until you're fitting the rings on the rod,

Measure the diameter of the rod where the new corks will go and ream out the centers of these corks with a rattail file. Use the method given earlier for measuring a rod when fitting a ferrule.

there's a good chance you won't get the holes true, which is easy to do while you have the edges of the rings to use as a reference line.

When the centers of the two new rings have been reamed out, cut each ring into two pieces (be sure to keep the proper pieces together). Make the cuts at an oblique rather than a right angle to the center of the rings; this will give your patched-in rings more strength. It's impossible to make just one cut and force the ring onto the rod butt. I've tried this shortcut several times, and every time the ring I was trying to force in cracked. Cork, among its other characteristics, is quite brittle. The picture shows the angle of the cuts you'll be making and the way the ring should look after being halved.

Put a generous coating of adhesive on every surface concerned: the bare section of rod, the flat surfaces of the rings still on the rod, the insides of the new rings where they will meet the rod, the angle cuts made when the rings were divided, and the tops and bottoms where the

This is how the new cork should look when divided. The bias cuts interlock better and have a little bit larger glue surface.

new rings will meet the old ones and each other. Then mate the new rings in the opening of the grip. If you've cut as shown and haven't been too ambitious in using the file or sandpaper in truing the old surfaces, the new rings will go into place reluctantly but tightly. Press all surfaces into good contact.

With heavy twine, wrap the mend as shown in the illustration. Put all the tension you can on the cord while wrapping; don't worry about it cutting into the new rings, because they've got to be sanded to match the contours of the grip. When the wrapping is in place, put the work aside to let the glue dry. In the job illustrated, I used Pliobond because I didn't have any waterproof resin glue mixed and wanted to get on with the job.

When the glue has set firm and you've taken off the wrap, your mended grip should look like the illustration, with the sharp shoulders of the new cork rings sticking out in a ridge at top and bottom. Use coarse sandpaper to reduce the new rings to the approximate contour

After applying glue to all surfaces that will touch another surface when the new rings are in place, set one ring on the rod and force the other into place. The cuts made in dividing the rings should not be in line lengthwise.

of the grip, then follow up by working over the entire grip with fine sandpaper as shown.

Although a lot of rodmakers recommend shaping cork grips on the rod, I've found that it's a lot easier to shape the grip separately and then fit it to the rod. Putting in a couple of new rings and sanding them to contour is one thing, but shaping an entire grip while turning the rod by hand is a very tedious proposition. I've tried the shaping-on-the-rod method when building rods, and even without guides to snag you as you turn the rod, it takes an hour or more to form a complete grip on the rod, while you can form one in ten minutes using a drill.

Wrap the grip as shown from about ¾ inch above to ¾ inch below the mend. Pull the wrapping cord as tight as possible.

Remove the wrapping when the glue has dried and reduce the shoulder formed by the new corks with coarse sandpaper. Work by rotating the grip on the sandpaper.

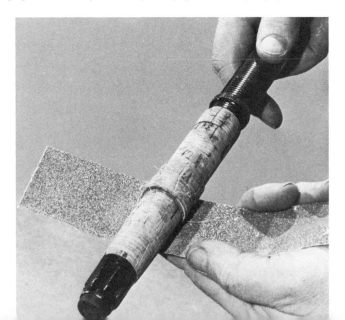

Splicing Broken Rods

This is the most exacting job you'll encounter on the list of repairs that are practical for the amateur. It's really not a hard job, but it does take some time and some careful measuring and sanding. It's a useful technique to learn, though, because it's the same method that you can use to update metal-ferruled rods and lighten them as well as improve their action by converting them to self-ferruled rods.

The one special tool that I've found almost indispensible in carrying out either this repair or the conversion is a warding file. This kind of file has one or more toothless sides, and makes filing an accurate right-angled joint easy and fast. A warding file, with a smooth face at right angles to a cutting face, enables you to file a true right angle, since the smooth or safe face rides along on the work without deepening the cut while the toothed face forms the angle. Machine shops still use warding files; so do newspapers that have Linotypes in the printing shop. If you can't find a warding file, you can make one by grinding the teeth off one of the narrow edges of a regular file. It's not a tool you'll need often, but it does make the job of splicing or plugging a fiberglass rod a lot easier.

Besides a file, the only tool you'll need is a saw. On the materials list, you'll need a section of a solid fiberglass rod of a diameter just a bit smaller than the inner diameter of the section of hollow rod you'll be splicing, epoxy glue, fine sandpaper, and a pencil. You'll also need a bit of patience. You can probably find a used solid fiberglass rod in a secondhand store, perhaps in a tackle shop. Discount houses usually have a bin full of solid glass rods at very low prices—a dollar or so.

As already noted, a crushed spot or break in a hollow fiberglass rod can be mended successfully only if it is 2 inches or less long. You can splice a rod that's been crushed over a bigger area, but taking out more than 2 to 2½ inches of a rod will change its action greatly, whereas a short splice will affect the rod's action only slightly. And, as also noted earlier, the upper 12 to 16 inches of a rod's tip cannot be spliced because in this area the inner diameter of the tube is too small to accommodate a sufficiently strong plug.

The first step in splicing a broken rod section is to remove the damaged area. This includes not just the portion that has been crushed,

Make the first saw cuts at the end of any splits that may have been caused by the break you are removing from the rod.

but any part on either side where longitudinal cracks radiating from the break have gone completely through the walls of the rod. In the accompanying picture, the saw blade is at the end of the cracked portion, the break in the rod can be seen to the right of the saw, and still farther to the right the dark area shows where the rod's finish has been removed up to the end of the cracks in that direction. The rod being repaired, incidentally, was caught in a slammed car door.

Remove the portion of the rod to the right of the major break that has been affected by cracks. After this has been done, the tip of an old solid glass rod is inserted in the lower piece of the hollow glass rod and a mark made on the solid rod at the point where it fills the inside of the broken piece of rod, as illustrated.

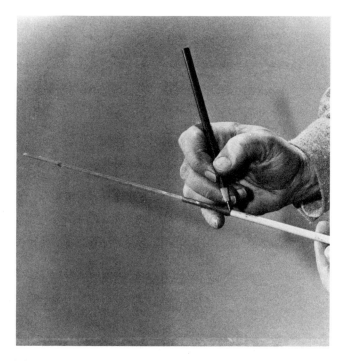

Slide a section of an old solid glass rod into the bottom piece of the tubular rod. Don't pound or force the solid glass rod, just slide it in until it stops, give it a gentle push to seat it, and mark it at the top of the saw cut.

Removed from the tube, the solid glass rod is sawed off about 1½ inches above the mark, and an equal distance below the mark. This 3-inch piece will form the plug or splicing support. Because a section of the hollow rod has been removed, there will be an interruption in the continuity of its taper in the upper portion. To compensate for this, the upper part of the plug must be reduced in diameter while its own taper is preserved. Do this with a file, rolling the plug on the file rather than holding it still and moving the file. Test the plug often as you work, inserting it in the upper piece of the hollow glass rod. When the plug begins to fit snugly in the upper piece, switch to sandpaper for the final reduction.

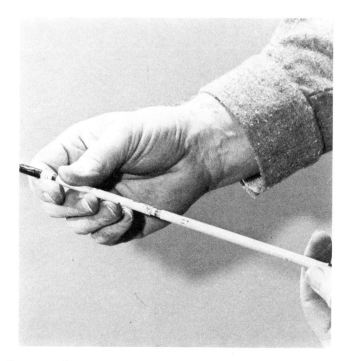

Don't try for a final fit at this stage. When the plug will slip into the tubular rod to within about ¼ inch of the mark, slide it into the bottom piece and check both pieces with the plug in place to be sure they will be in alignment when they are finally joined.

As soon as the top piece of the hollow rod fits to within about ¼ inch of the plug's center mark, stop sanding and put the plug in the lower piece of the hollow rod. You'll find that it will slip past your center mark by perhaps ⅛ to ¼ inch; this is normal and nothing to worry about. Try the upper piece of the broken rod on the plug; there should be a gap of about ½ inch between the two ends of the broken rod pieces when they are joined tight, as the illustration shows.

Separate the pieces of rod and push the plug back down the tube of the lower piece. Apply a thick coating of epoxy to the inner wall of the lower or larger piece of the broken rod. If you put adhesive on the

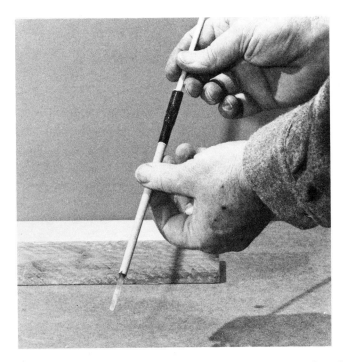

Insert the plug in the bottom piece of the tubular rod and push it into place with a dowel. Don't force it, just seat it firmly. The center mark on the plug will be ⅛ to ¼ inch above the edge of the tubular rod, this is normal.

plug, it will leave an epoxy trail all the way up the tube when inserted.

Slip the plug into the bottom piece of the broken rod section and seat it with a piece of dowel or with the sawed-off tip of the solid glass rod. Don't force the plug into place, use firm but gentle pressure. The glue inside the hollow rod will now flow around the plug, and it will go in no farther than the original mark made when it was first fitted. Put the glued piece aside now and wait for the epoxy to set completely before continuing work.

When the glue joint is dry, get out your warding file, if you've been able to find one, or use a regular smooth file to carry the taper of the plug back to the end of the hollow rod. Test the work frequently by

When the glue dries, work down the upper part of the plug with file and sandpaper to fit snugly into the top piece of the tubular rod.

slipping the upper piece of the hollow rod over the plug; it should fit snugly without wobbling or turning loosely on the plug. When you're satisfied with the fit of the upper piece of rod on the plug, coat the plug with epoxy and set the upper piece of rod into place, then wipe off the excess glue.

There will be a tiny shoulder where the two pieces of the hollow glass rod meet. Don't file it smooth, but wrap the splice with thread to match the other wrappings on the rod, overwrapping above the shoulder to get a smooth finish. If you prefer, you can fair the two sections at the splice with a tiny bit of epoxy glue applied in a line just above the shoulder and smoothed with a toothpick or splinter of wood to conceal the joint and make a smooth taper; the glue will be hidden by the wrapping.

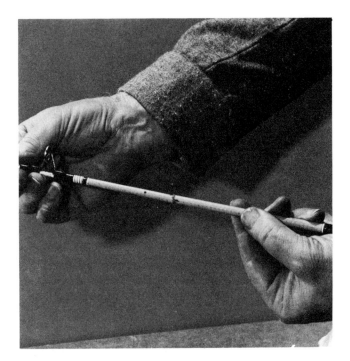

Slide the plug into the upper piece of the tubular rod and wipe off excess epoxy. There will be a small shoulder where the pieces meet. Leave a bit of epoxy when you wipe, and use a toothpick as a trowel to taper the glue above the shoulder so the splice will be easier to wrap after the glue dries.

If you're splicing the butt section of a broken hollow glass rod, you must remove the grip in order for the bottom plug to be fitted. This plug-splicing technique, when stopped at the point where the two broken pieces of rod are permanently joined by applying epoxy to the upper part of the plug, can be used to make a self-ferruled rod. In this conversion, you should wrap both the upper and lower pieces of the hollow glass rod with winding thread, starting as close as possible to the point where they meet over the plug. A double wrap, or a wrap with heavier thread than you would normally use, is a good idea. When finishing off the wrap in a rod converted by this method, use one of the epoxy winding lacquers instead of varnish and apply two or three coats, to further strengthen the ends of the hollow glass rod.

Repairing HMG Rods

Any major repair to an HMG rod should be done in the manufacturer's own shop. Fenwick, one of the pioneers of HMG rodmaking and one of the two firms having complete facilities for making these rods from blank-molding to final fitting, advises that not only are the tapers and ferrules on their HMG rods molded and mated by methods that can't be duplicated in home workshops, but that they use special adhesives of their own formulation in making their HMG rods.

Your own repair work on an HMG rod should be limited to such minor jobs as replacing a guide or tip-top, or, at most, putting on a new grip. This will not always be the case, of course. As the use of HMG rods spreads and the technology involved in their construction becomes simplified—and as more data is accumulated about them through the shared experiences of anglers using them—it will be possible for the home craftsman to take on major jobs of repairing and rebuilding them.

Repairing Bamboo Rods

While a majority of anglers who came to the sport after 1950 have never used a bamboo rod, and tend to look on them as quaintly anachronistic, even as antiques, the bamboo rod is very much alive. Understandably, the literature concerning its care and repair is not. This is unfortunate, because there are a lot of fine bamboos still around, most of them tucked away in some half-remembered storage space. If taken out, refurbished, and used, these rods can give anglers a very unique fishing experience.

Although the working life of even the finest bamboo rod is limited, few rods are ever used to this limit by their original owners. Among my own bamboos, I have rods made as long ago as 1935, which have been little-used, and which still retain their life and action. I also have a few that have been used to their limit, but to which I cling because of the memories they bring back when I take them out of their cases and handle them. If you run across a bamboo rod that looks dilapidated and worn out, don't judge it on the basis of looks alone. Joint it up, put a matching line on it, and try it out. You may be pleasantly surprised.

When you do find a good but old bamboo, it will undoubtedly need some working over. With only a few minor variations, the same procedures and techniques used in repairing tubular glass rods apply to repairs on bamboo rods. The methods of replacing guides, ferrules, reel seats, and grips are identical, although you will probably want to use adhesives other than epoxy in working with bamboo. Thermosetting stick ferrule cement or rubber-based liquid cement are equally satisfactory choices.

One major difference between bamboo and glass rods is that all bamboo rods must be varnished for their entire length. Bamboo is susceptible to water damage, and a thin coating of varnish is required to protect it. When beginning to renew an old bamboo rod, your first job after taking off its guides will be to remove the varnish. This is best done with a small cabinetmaker's scraper, working with light pressure along the flat sides of the rod, taking care not to gouge into the surface of the rod.

Bamboo rods are made of glued-up triangular strips, and the working strength of bamboo is concentrated in its tough outer fibers, which form the outside of all bamboo rods. Because they are only a few thousandths of an inch thick, and are very susceptible to damage by nicks or cuts, work your scraper with a light hand when removing the varnish.

After the scraping has taken off the heaviest varnish coating, there will still be an unseen residue remaining on the rod. Polish it with crocus cloth—and I use the word "polish" rather than "sand," because you don't want to use even the finest sandpaper. The crocus cloth will remove the varnish residue without cutting into the bamboo's fibers.

Many older bamboo rods take on a slight curve as they age or are used. This curve, or set, can be removed and the rod straightened after the varnish has been removed. Put an inch or so of water in a teakettle

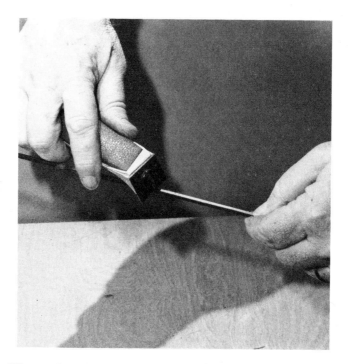

When using a scraper to remove varnish from a bamboo rod, work the blade flat on the flat sides without cutting into the corners. Handle the scraper with a light hand to avoid nicking or cutting into the bamboo's surface.

and bring it to a boil. When steam starts pouring out of the spout, pass the curved portion of the rod back and forth in the steam for three or four minutes, never longer than five minutes at one time, and gently flex the rod section with your fingers, bending it against the curve, starting at the center and working alternately toward the ends. You might need to apply steam two or three times, but with gentle persistent pressure the set can be removed and the curved portion straightened. Lay the rod section flat to cool and dry out.

Chances are that any bamboo rod that you're apt to find today is one by a good craftsman; cheap bamboos abounded, but few of them were ever considered by their owners as being worth saving. Better-

A pin punch will drive the pins out far enough to grasp them with pliers and pull them free. Support the rod as shown, between wood blocks.

grade bamboo rods were always fitted with welted nickel silver ferrules, and most rodmakers who worked in bamboo also pinned their ferrules with a short length of nickel silver wire driven through holes in the ferrule and polished off even with its surface. These pins must be removed before the ferrules can be taken off the rod. Use a fine pin punch—the one shown in the picture is made from a dartboard dart—and with the tip of the rod supported between wood blocks, tap the punch gently until the opposite end of the ferrule is driven out of its hole. It can then be grasped with pliers and pulled out.

Occasionally, a ferrule on an old rod stored without being unjointed will be frozen so tightly that even the four-handed unjointing method described earlier won't part it. The only thing to be done in such a case is to take the rod sections out of the ferrules—practically all bamboo rods have ferrules set with heat-sensitive adhesives—and use a dowel to tap the male end of the ferrule out of the female end. The end of the male ferrule can then be polished with crocus cloth to remove the oxidation, which is the cause of its freezing.

Most high-quality bamboo rods are also fitted with marked ferrules, a tiny pinprick on the welt of the female and the shoulder of the male ferrule to show how the sections should be jointed up. Use these marks to guide you in reassembling the rod, when you are replacing its guides and other components.

Since bamboo rods are hexagonal instead of round in cross section, grips that are being replaced should be reamed inside with a triangular or square file instead of a rattail to get a better fit on the rod. And, since ferrules are round, the ends of rod sections where they are fitted were rounded by the maker to enter the barrel of the ferrule. Try not to reduce the diameter of these ends when working on a bamboo rod. If you do, use the tissue paper technique described earlier to build them up again, or use heavy rod winding thread or ravelled-out pieces of soft cotton twine to fill the gap.

After all the guides have been replaced, and the rod is ready to be varnished, take the extra step used by master rodbuilders to achieve a perfect finish. With a piece of felt—a chunk cut out of an old hat is excellent—polish the rod vigorously. This gives an ultrasmooth surface that will accept varnish perfectly. And, instead of applying the varnish with a brush, warm it slightly and wipe it on with a soft lintless cloth. A few custom rodbuilders even scorn using a rag, and apply a microscopically thin coat of varnish with their bare fingers. They put on a second coat in this same manner after the first coat has dried and the rod has been rubbed down with rottenstone.

Only a handful of craftsmen are still making bamboo rods today, but a lot of the rods made by early masters such as Gillum, Payne, Phillipson, Young, Powell, Leonard, Orvis, Winston, and Thomas are still in existence. If you're lucky enough to discover a rod by any early maker, your reward in restoring it to its original condition may be doubled. Not only will you have an example of what is probably the most exacting hand-crafted workmanship ever done, but if you're very lucky the rod you restore will have enough life left in it to give you a new and exciting fishing experience when you use it.

Once you've gotten into rod repairing and restoring, acquired the feel of handling fittings and wrapping thread and cork, you'll find that doing this kind of work is not just an enjoyable pastime, but one that repays you with tackle that you're sure will be capable of good performance in addition to looking good.

3

REELS

Reels over the years have steadily grown more complex, and unlike rods depend less on individual artisanship in their design and manufacture than they do on precision parts and assembly techniques. For this reason, a lot of anglers hesitate to strip down a reel to perform the simple but vital maintenance jobs of oiling and cleaning. The result is that a lot of reels have an unnecessarily shortened life.

Reels have come a long way since primitive man first cast his heavy woven-bark lines from a crude shuttle or bobbin held in his hand. Even in the days of Dame Juliana Berners and Izaac Walton, rods were not always equipped with reels. Anglers of that era used a braided horsehair line the length of their rod, and the line, tied to the rod tip, was cast by the rod being lifted and the line laid out with a sweeping overhand flipping movement. Even after the invention of the rigid line guide made casting possible, reels continued to be little more than storage spools that performed no function in casting.

First of what can be described as "modern" reels appeared on fly rods in the 1800s. Earlier reels were simply grooved flat wooden spools with a peg for an axle and a nubbin of a handle, and were attached at right angles to the rod instead of parallel to it. Reels of this type, improved by the use of metal and other materials, are still in use today; witness the Pflueger Sal-Trout reel, used for trolling wire lines.

Multiplying reels are the contribution of the United States to angling. A Kentucky watchmaker, George Snyder, made a reel in 1806 that would enable him to cast minnows from a boat floating along a stream and drop the minnow into the brushy shoreline where black bass lurked. Snyder used gears from clocks and watches to create a gear train that turned the reel spool twice for each revolution of the handle, which doubled the number of casts he could make in a given period by reducing the length of time required to reel the minnow back to his boat. Snyder's reel was fragile and needed frequent repairs, but it worked, and friends began to demand reels like it.

Between 1806 and 1818, Snyder made only a few reels. Nobody knows how many of his hand-crafted creations ever existed, but it may have been as few as eighteen or twenty. Around 1817 or 1818, one of Snyder's reels found its way into the hands of another watchmaker, Jonathan Meek, and Meek improved the reel by strengthening its mechanism and revising its gearing to give three revolutions of the spool for each turn of the handle. Meek's improvements were so successful that he began building his version commercially, and may have turned out as many as 150, a large number for that period. Then, Benjamin Milam, a metalworking artisan, used the Snyder–Meek reel as a model for an even more compact and sturdier version that he put into production in 1820—a production run that was to continue for over 100 years.

On the other side of the Atlantic, the Hardy brothers in England evolved—primarily for their own use—a fly-fisherman's reel that had a metal frame and spool and feet that allowed it to be attached to the rod in a parallel plane. As was the case with Snyder and Meek, friends of the Hardys clamored for duplicates, and by 1872 the Hardys were in the business of making their reels commercially. The business they began almost by accident is still making very good fishing reels today.

About the time the Hardys were setting up their plant, another Briton and angling enthusiast, Holden Illingworth, was standing one day watching cotton threads running off the spinning bobbins of the cotton mill he operated. Illingworth thought, why not a reel that would allow fishing line to flow off its end and be retrieved by a bail, as these bobbins are? It took him several years of spare-time work to transform his idle thought into a working reel, but by the mid-1890s he had produced the first spinning reel—the derivation of the name is obvious—and the reel was put into commercial production in the early 1900s. Perhaps without realizing it, Illingworth had gone back in his reel to those first used by primitive man, whose lines flowed off their shuttles in the same fashion that it flows off the fixed spool of a modern spinning reel.

Oddly, that spinning reel didn't cross the ocean to the United States for more than a half-century after it was first put into manufacture. It was the 1940s before spinning tackle began to be widely used in the United States. The instant popularity it attained then resulted in the open-face spinning reel being converted by United States designers into the closed-face version that today is called the spincasting reel, and is perhaps the reel used more than any other kind by present-day anglers.

A major contribution to modern reel development was made in the early days of the present century by Julius vom Hofe. Vom Hofe was a maker of custom deep-sea reels, beefed-up and immensely strengthened versions of the original Snyder–Meek–Milam baitcasting reel. It was Vom Hofe who got the idea for a mechanism that could be added to his reels, one that would be an equalizing factor between the heavy plunges of an ocean monster and the line retrieving of an excited angler.

Vom Hofe's device consisted of a series of leather discs that could be squeezed together or relieved of pressure by adjusting a cup-shaped spring. The friction of the discs against each other could be regulated by the spring's tension adjustment to apply a controllable amount of pressure or drag on the line. Coupled with the washer and spring arrangement was a lever that disengaged the gears driven by the reel's handle when the pull (or drag) on the line exceeded the amount for which the spring tension had been preset. The device was adjusted by a flattened knob under the handle of the reel, and this knob was shaped like a five-pointed star, hence the term "star drag."

Later, the device was modified to include a separate lever that when thrown removed the reel's spool from contact with the handle's gears and allowed the spool to play out line without the handle turning. In modified form, but with the basic principle of controlled friction applied through a series of washers retained, Vom Hofe's star drag is used on many of today's freshwater baitcasting reels. It is also incorporated in one form or another in all spinning and spincasting reels as well as on the geared fly reels used for heavy salmon fishing and saltwater fly-fishing.

Reels are often described in terms of retrieve ratio. This simply indicates the number of turns the spool makes with each revolution of the handle. Most fly reels are operated by a handle attached to the spool, and one turn of the handle equals one turn of the spool, which gives the reel a 1:1 ratio. Most freshwater spinning reels of the open-face type usually have a retrieve ratio between 4:1 and 5:1; saltwater spinning reels will normally have a 3:1 or 3.5:1 ratio. The most common ratio for closed-face spincasting reels is 4:1. Baitcasting reel ratios run from 3.5:1 to 4.5:1, and the retrieve ratios on big saltwater reels usually run between 2.5:1 and 3:1.

In spite of all the advances made in reel design, construction, and the improved metals and plastics that go into reel components, fishing reels of today and of angling's recent yesterdays still have more similarities than differences. All reels basically consist of a frame, a spool, and a handle or crank. The frame supports the axle on which the spool revolves—or in the case of spinning and spincast reels, revolves the spool—and the frame also provides anchorage for a foot with which the reel is attached to the rod. The spool holds the line, and though often operating through a chain of gears, the handle turns the spool.

To these basics, of course, many refinements have been added: star drag, free spool, level-wind, centrifugal brakes on baitcasting reels. However, even the refinements are similar, not because the design staff of one manufacturer copies the work of another, but because everyone who sets out to design a reel must operate within the same limitations of weight, function, and the materials from which a reel's components are fabricated. There are also certain laws of mechanics that govern gearing that have not changed since ancient times. By the very nature of these limitations, one designer inevitably is led to basically the same conclusions arrived at by his fellows and to a very similar resolution.

There is, of course, a certain amount of cross-licensing of patents in the tackle industry, just as there is among the makers of automobiles and electronic equipment. A breakthrough by Manufacturer A is exploited by him in his products for several years, then for a fee, Manufacturer B is licensed to use the breakthrough device on his equipment. So are Manufacturers C, D, and E. After all, B, C, D, or E might come up some day with a device that A might want to use on his equipment. And the ultimate beneficiaries of these agreements are the anglers who use the products of all the manufacturers.

The point is that there's a strong resemblance between the reels of Brand A and those of Brands B, C, D, and E because of cross-licensing of patents as well as because of the laws of mechanics and physics. What this means is that you don't have to be intimately familiar with every model of reel made by every manufacturer in order to maintain and perform minor repairs on most reels of the same type. In all the reel families, there are more similarities than differences. If you can handle a typical fly reel, spinning reel, spincasting reel, and baitcasting reel of one make, you can probably handle those of other makes. And, as complicated as a modern reel may seem to be, the chief things a reel needs are regular cleaning and lubricating. If you take care of these two simple chores, you'll seldom have a broken reel to repair.

The cause of most reel breakage and damage is simple neglect. Improper use—using a line far heavier than the maximum test recommended for a given model of reel or using monofilament on a reel with a spool designed to handle only braided line—is the second most frequent cause of reel damage. Accidents hold third place; component failures due to defective parts or assembly errors come in fourth. In about 4 percent of all reels returned for service, manufacturer's shop repairmen are unable to determine the reason for breakage.

Normal wear and tear incurred by long use is another important cause of reel failures, but proper and regular cleaning and lubrication would eliminate or greatly reduce the damage caused by time and use. As one manufacturer has stated, "The more complicated reels need regular attention far more than do the simpler types such as fly reels."

It's pretty obvious that a lot of fishermen who wouldn't go more than ten miles or two days past an oil change due in their cars aren't as aware that regular oil changes are needed by their reels, too. It's also apparent that far too many anglers pay very little attention to the instruction booklets that are included with every reel sold. It's understandable that a fisherman buying a reel second-hand might not be informed about the maintenance needs of that reel, since the original owner probably glanced at the instruction booklet and tossed it aside. But all manufacturers will provide instruction leaflets even to anglers who've bought their products from a friend or at a second-hand store or garage sale. And all makers have Customer Service Departments that will reply to specific queries about reel care.

If your reel needs a replacement part, you can be pretty sure it will be available. A majority of manufacturers make extra parts during their production runs for a given model, and most of them maintain parts stocks for six years or longer. In my survey of reel manufacturers, only two quoted shorter periods for parts availability, and even those two indicated they keep a stock of parts for two years and four years, respectively. One firm, the Johnson Reel Company, in replying to the question of how long a supply of parts for all models of their reels is maintained, noted simply "Forever."

A growing number of reelmakers now maintain factory service depots in different parts of the country. Others have training programs for independent tackle repairmen who learn how to do necessary work in their own shops. And all reelmakers indicated they will provide parts direct to customers, though two require that the customer order pass through a dealer's store.

Despite the fact that getting a reel repaired is becoming progressively easier, it is much less trouble to keep your reels operating perfectly than it is to have them fixed. That's why maintenance is so terribly important.

Maintenance Needs Common to All Reels

Whether it's a massive 16/0 saltwater reel or a tiny, delicate ultralight spinning reel, your reel needs at least a minimum amount of care. Wherever metal meets metal, as it does in many places in a complex modern reel, a drop of oil or dab of grease today saves a broken or damaged part tomorrow.

To keep water out of the reel's vitals, most manufacturers provide oiling ports with a cap of some kind, and this tends to cause many anglers to forget that these exterior oiling points exist. Not all reels need to be stripped to oil them, and many can be kept clean without the need to do more than to slip the spool out now and then and wipe vulnerable parts with an oily cloth. Of course, every reel should be taken apart at least once a year—oftener, if it gets regular and hard use—and be given a thorough cleaning.

Most manufacturers specify the lubricants they feel best suited for use with their reels, and many of them supply a small quantity of the recommended oil or light grease with the reel when it is purchased. A number of manufacturers also have lubricants produced to their own specifications, and most of these will work as well on one reel as on the next. Typically, reel lubricants are a lightweight oil or grease containing a water-repellant, and a rust or corrosion inhibitor, which are seldom found in lubricants designed for all-purpose use.

If your reel is accidentally dunked, don't depend entirely on the water-repellant in the lubricant you use on it to keep all the water away from all the parts. Usually, a dunked reel can be freed of most water just by giving it a few good shakes, and you can go on using it until the end of the fishing day. But then you should strip it and clean it and renew its lubricant. If a reel has been underwater for several minutes, it's a good idea to remove one of the side plates and the spool and give the gears and bearings a chance to dry.

Prolonged storage will often thicken reel lubricants to the point where they lose effectiveness; moreover, such storage can actually cause damage. All oils and greases tend to oxidize and thicken when exposed to air. Gummy grease or oil will not only show up in slowed-down action of a baitcasting reel, but in a "hard" retrieve. That spare reel on your storage shelf or in your tackle box that you carry only for emergencies and seldom use needs regular attention as much as does the reel you use on every fishing trip.

Each reel has points of special vulnerability. The open construction characteristic of most fly reels allows grit and sandy particles to work into the open space between spool and frame and to collect on the sideplate. Simply slipping out the spool and wiping the inner face of spool and reel cures this. Baitcasting reels have a smaller gap between spool and sideplates, but this gap is wide enough to collect water sprayed from a wet line when the spool spins during a cast. Saltwater reels, even though made of rust-resistant metals, are especially vulnerable to this kind of wetting, and should be cleaned oftener than freshwater reels because of salt water's greater corrosive nature.

Most of today's baitcasting reels have some kind of level-wind device, and its exposed worm gear is a notorious collector of grit. This gear can usually be cleaned without stripping the reel by using a pipe cleaner or toothpick dipped in kerosene or alcohol. Spinning reels are vulnerable to grit in the area just beneath the spool, and regular cleaning of this part of the reel involves no more trouble than slipping the spool out and wiping the area beneath it with an oily cloth or pipe cleaner.

Spinning reels have another type of vulnerability that lies in the field of misuse, and is a matter of prevention rather than maintenance. With few exceptions, open-face spinning reels are designed to perform most efficiently with monofilament in a limited range of weight, or test. An ultralight spinning reel, for instance, simply isn't engineered to handle 20-pound monofilament; the heaviest line that should be used on such a reel is about 4-pound test. A majority of standard-size spinning reels will handle mono in the range of 6 to 15 pounds without strain, though they operate most efficiently when filled with 8- or 10-pound test mono. Heavy-duty saltwater reels are designed to handle mono ranging from 15- to 50-pound test, but they, too, function best when spooled with mono in the 20- to 30-pound range.

Almost all professional reel repairmen are very emphatic about the danger of overloading spinning reels with too-heavy monofilament. One of them explained it this way: "There are a lot of fishermen who still don't realize that spinning reels are designed for light-line fishing. They think a spinning reel, like a baitcasting reel, can handle any test line from 10 to 50 pounds, but that simply isn't the case. A too-heavy line strains a reel much more severely than playing the heaviest fish. It overworks not only the drag but the main gears as well, and the first thing I look for when a reel is brought in for repairs is the weight mono on it. Nine times out of ten, I find the reel is loaded with line too heavy for it to handle."

Spincast reels, which are very much like open-face reels in some features of their design, are seldom overloaded because their spools accommodate only a limited range of mono diameters. It's almost impossible to put 20- or 30-pound test mono on a spincast reel designed to take only 8- to 12-pound test. But when a spincast reel is over-strained, it shows the effects even more quickly than does its open-face cousin.

Overloading of baitcasting reels can also occur, especially when an older reel designed to be used with braided line is loaded with monofilament. Mono began to be widely used on baitcasting reels only in the 1960s, and it took a while for manufacturers to catch up with the trend and design spools engineered for mono use. Braided casting line is rough in comparison with monofilament; when reeled in the friction of its surface causes it to maintain a fixed position on the spool. Slick monofilament has virtually no surface friction, and as more line is reeled in it presses down between the layers of line already on the spool. This creates a side-to-side pressure that causes reel spools to crack unless they have been designed to resist this outward pressure. Most baitcasting reels made since 1967 or 1968 have spools designed to handle mono, and depending on make and model, many older reels can be equipped with these new spools. A new spool is the only cure for this problem, by the way.

If you still have doubts about your ability to strip down a reel, either for maintenance or repairs, perhaps the following sections will convince you that reels aren't really as complicated as you think.

Fly Reels

Simplest of all reels are those used by the freshwater fly-fishermen. Though there are geared fly reels, used in fishing offshore and for such giants as tarpon in brackish water and salmon in heavy-running streams, their maintenance and repairs must be classed with those connected with baitcasting reels, which their mechanisms strongly resemble.

An average fly reel will have only three or four components in addition to its basic frame and spool. About 99.9 percent of all fly reels have handles integral with the spool, and their mechanism consists only of a gear that engages a rachet to keep the spool from turning of its own momentum, and perhaps a thumbscrew-type friction brake that

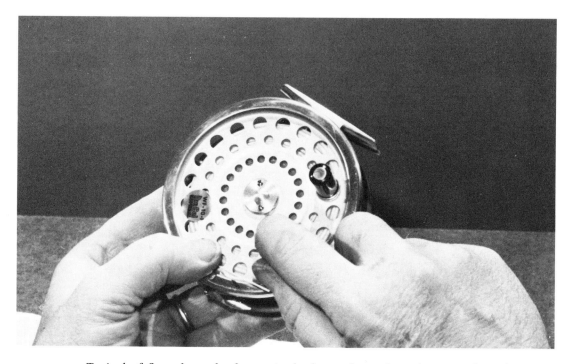

Typical of fly rod spool releases is the lever above the axle as used on the Hardy-made Scientific Anglers System reels.

presses on a shoulder at the back of the spool to allow an adjustment of the tension required to strip off line. The axle that goes through the spool is usually integral with the frame.

Most fly reels can be stripped simply by releasing a catch; in the Scientific Anglers fly reels like the one shown, the catch is a lever that sticks out of the axle cover. When the spool is lifted out, all necessary service or repair operations can be carried out. The only oiling point requiring attention is the axle, which requires a single drop of oil now and then. The eccentric cam directly below the axle is the drag adjustment, and if the reel is used for left-hand operation this part must be reversed. Reassembly is simply a matter of snapping the spool back into the frame.

A pushbutton releases the spool on many reels, such as the Pflueger Medalist, the South Bend Purist, the Shakespeare Finalist,

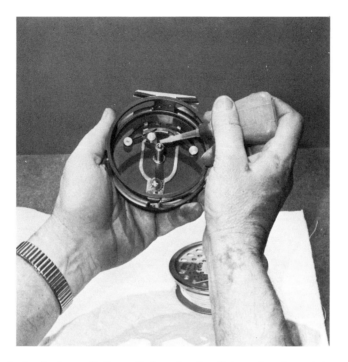

A single drop of oil applied to the tip of the axle, plus wiping the inner surface of the sideplate with a lightly oiled cloth, is all the service this reel requires.

Fly reels modeled on the Pflueger Medalist have a pushbutton spool release above the axle.

A dab of light reel grease should be applied to reels of this type along the upper part of the axle.

and several models of fly reels by Berkley and Heddon. Again, the only oiling point is the axle, which requires a tiny dab of reel grease. The thumbscrew at the top of the reel controls the drag, which is the rectangular fiber piece with a circular cutout that is located just above the axle.

Fly reels that don't have a lever or pushbutton release for their spool will have a screw-type spool release. Usually, the screw slot is wide enough so that a dime can be used if the reel has to be opened in the field. Inside, the Laurentian reel—a Canadian copy of the early Hardys—has the typically simple fly-reel mechanism, a triangular metal piece at top left in the frame is spring-loaded and is the antireverse; the click is a similar piece at the lower right. This picture was taken before the reel was wiped clean and shows the accumulated grit

This Canadian-made Laurentian, modeled after early Hardy reels, typifies the simplicity of most fly reels. A single pawl at left is operated by a button on the outer face of the sideplate; this click on–click off arrangement is the only adjustment the reel has. The pawl and spring at upper right are spares and can be installed without tools. As the photo shows, the reel badly needs cleaning. Lubrication is a dab of grease on the upper part of the axle.

on the sideplate that will eventually cause excessive wear if not removed.

There's really not much that can go wrong with a fly reel, except a broken spring in the click or antireverse devices, and replacement of these can usually be made with no tool other than a screwdriver—sometimes with no tool but your fingers.

105

Open-face Spinning Reels

Spinning reels fall into two major categories of design and construction. To begin with, all open-face spinning reels are technically known as "fixed-spool" reels because these spools are fixed to their shafts. Line is retrieved by a bail or fingers on the housing, which revolves instead of the spool. Primary terms used in describing gears are "ring gear" to describe a plain round gear, "pinion" to describe the smaller of two gears in a linkage, and "teeth" being matched projections by which the gears react with one another.

Four basic gearing arrangements are common to all spinning reels. The simplest is the direct drive, in which the teeth of both ring and pinion are on their outer rims and the two gears are on the same parallel plane with their shafts also parallel. The second arrangement is the spiral bevel pinion drive, in which gear and pinion meet at an angle of 90 degrees and their shafts are at 90 degrees to one another; the teeth on the ring gear in this arrangement are slanted on a side of its rim rather than the edge and the teeth of both ring and pinion are cut in an arc which if extended would form a spiral. A variation of this is the hypoid pinion gear arrangement in which the shaft of the pinion is not in the same center line as the shaft of the ring, but is offset to one side or the other. This is the same gear arrangement used in most automobile rear axles because it is stronger and operates more quietly than the straight spiral bevel gear setup.

The fourth gear arrangement is the cross-axis helical, in which ring and pinion meet on a parallel plane but with the axis of their shafts crossing but not intersecting at right angles in the center of each gear. In this arrangement the pinion looks like it's riding pickaback on the ring or clinging to the underside of the ring. If all this sounds confusing, it will clear up when you see the pictures of the actual gears in the actual reels.

Basically, the circular motion created when you turn the handle of any spinning reel must be transmitted by one of the four gear arrangements described to the spool shaft, which is at right angles to the handle. The shaft must also be given a secondary back-and-forth movement to wind the line evenly on the spool during a retrieve. Some reels have a gear, others a cam, which does this. We're not concerned

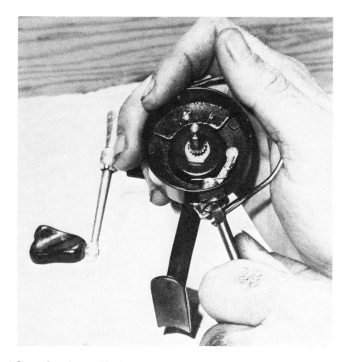

After slipping off the spool of Garcia's light-duty open-face Mitchell spinning reel, the first part removed in stripping the reel is the bail. It can be lifted off after taking out its retaining screw.

about the drag mechanism on spinning reels, because it's inside the line spool and adjusted by a knob on the spool. A damaged spool is replaced instead of being repaired.

Stripping a spinning reel begins with removing the spool. In the lightweight Garcia Mitchell model pictured, the spool is held by twin latches at the top of the shaft. Next, the bail-retaining screw is taken out. Below the bail is a tension spring, and after the bail is off this spring can be lifted out by catching its upper coil with the tip of a screwdriver blade. In this model reel, a single screw holds the side-plate; the front edge of the plate is anchored by a channel cut in a raised section of the frame below the spool.

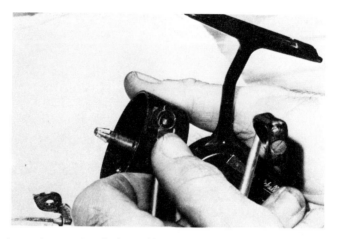

A tension spring below the bail is lifted from its housing with the tip of a screwdriver.

One screw and a retaining slot just below the center of the spool cup hold the sideplate in place; removing the screw allows the sideplate to be pulled out.

Gearing is the spiral bevel pinion type. The ring gear at the bottom of the housing is attached directly to the handle and meshes with a pinion on the spool shaft directly under the spool cup. Inner teeth on the ring gear operate the spring-loaded yoke running to the rear of the shaft and move it back and forth. The oval cover plate in the center of the ring gear must be removed for servicing and lubricating. After lifting off the cover plate and cleaning, a dab of light reel grease goes in each socket of the cover plate and another in the cup on the rear shaft housing. A drop of grease at any point on the ring gear will lubricate the entire gear assembly. Never overlubricate a light-duty reel.

Removing the sideplate reveals the gearing. A spiral bevel gear is shown, the ring gear's teeth meshing with a pinion on the shaft. Inner teeth on the ring mesh with pinions on the twin shafts of the yoke to move the spool back and forth. A cover plate in the center, shown being removed in one of the photos, is taken out to clean the grease cup

To show the great similarity between reels of this type, look at the gearing exposed by removing the right-hand cover plate of a different reel. Except for size of the ring and pinion, the gearing is identical.

and lubricate the reel. A dab of lubricant should be put in the cup of the housing located at the rear of the shaft. Removing the second sideplate disengages and takes out the main gear, and also releases the studs that hold the rear shaft housing, which can then be removed and any broken part of the mechanism replaced.

To show the similarity of spinning reels of the same type, the left sideplate of a different model Garcia reel has been removed to show the main gear, which is simply lifted out of the plate for cleaning or replacement. The studs holding the shaft housing are shown; they are located on either side of the housing near the frame. The buttons in the sideplate to the left of the main gear and immediately above and below it secure these studs and keep the housing in place when the gear is assembled.

Reassembling a reel is easy to do if you keep the parts in order by placing them at one side of the work area in a series of lines, putting each part in place as it is removed. Then, when you begin reassembling, you simply pick up each component in the reverse order from which it was laid down. By doing this you can quickly reassemble even an unfamiliar reel.

Now let's look at a spinning reel of the second type, one having a crossed-axis shaft gearing and an eccentric cam that provides the in-and-out motion to the spool. The reel is a Quick Finessa, one of the few spinning reels that can easily be switched from right-hand to left-hand operation. The method of removing the spool is slightly different—a pushbutton in the stem unlocks the spool. The base of the shaft shown in the picture has an accumulation of caked grease that should be cleaned out with a brush dipped in kerosene before new lubricant is applied. The bottom of the spool cup shows bits of grit that need to be wiped away also.

To remove the sideplate, the oiling port plate must first be taken off. With the sideplate removed, the gearing is exposed, as is the cam, the curved piece of metal that arcs across the upper part of the picture connecting gear and shaft. The ''L'' on the plate is to mark the cam as being for left-hand operation. With these reels, right-hand and left-hand cams are provided and in converting them the cams must be changed. The cam marked ''R'' would be placed on the other side of the gear. The main, and only, gear is removed with a screwdriver, the nut holding it to the handle can be seen just under the upper end of the cam. Shakespeare and Heddon spinning reels use a similar drive arrangement.

The interior design of both the yoke and cam type spinning reels is very straightforward, their stripping and assembly quite simple. Trouble is easy to spot. Once either sideplate has been removed, the main gear and shaft gears can be inspected for broken teeth or bending; the friction points where hardened grease might cause sluggishness or freezing can be spotted as easily. Replacing a broken or damaged part

A different gearing system will be seen in this Quick Finessa. The first step in stripping any reel is removing the spool. In this reel, an important service point is the shaft housing at the bottom of the spool cup.

A service port on the sideplate of this reel does double duty; it gives access to the gears for servicing and when the reel is shifted from right-hand to left-hand operation the plate is moved to the right side.

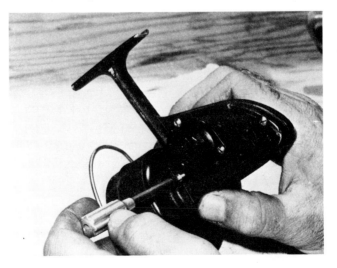

This reel and others noted in the text are crossed-axis geared. The rim-toothed ring is attached to the handle shaft and meshes with a helical pinion on the spool shaft. Back-and-forth motion of the spool shaft is provided by the curved cam attached eccentrically to the ring gear.

is usually a simple matter of lifting out the part and slipping in a new one. At most, you will need to take out one or two retaining studs or screws, with your fingers or tweezers or a screwdriver.

Accidental damage, such as that caused by dropping a reel on a hard surface, seldom affects the mechanism of a reel. Such things as a bent bail or a broken handle can be replaced without any detailed instructions. Damage to the frame is another matter, however. If the foot is broken off, or if the spool cup is cracked or a piece broken out of it, a new frame will be called for, since most spinning reel frames are of a light metal such as aluminum or magnesium, and making small, precise welds in these metals is beyond the skill of most welding shops.

Accidents can and do happen to anybody. Even the most careful angler will drop his tackle to save himself a fall, and count himself lucky if the only damage done is to his gear. Misuse and neglect are not accidents, though, and the damage they cause is preventable.

Spincast Reels

These are often called closed-face spinning reels, because while they are designed for free-line, fixed-spool casting, their spools are enclosed in a rounded or conical metal shell with a line entry opening in its center. Under this is a second dome or cone, usually made of soft, pliable plastic, over which the line runs to the side of the spool cup. Here it is engaged by one or two small metal or ceramic-coated pins that catch the line during a retrieve and pass it to the spool. These pins or fingers retract when a cast is being made; they are the equivalent of the curved bail on an open-face reel. The spool of a spincast reel is usually quite narrow, which eliminates the need for it to travel back and forth to distribute retrieved line evenly.

Most closed-face reels use a hypoid gear train to transmit the turning of the handle to a shaft that is connected with the pickup pins. Most spincast reels now have a thumb-brake lever or button at their back that is coupled to the inner dome or to a separate ring fitted with a washer of soft plastic that pinches the line against the outer metal dome to stop its flow off the reel. In some spincast reels, the soft inner plastic dome functions as a drag as well as a brake, but the larger models are fitted with a conventional washer-type drag adjusted by a star-plate under the handle or a thumbscrew on the frame of the reel.

Stripping a spincast reel is very simple. The first step is to remove the front cover plate; most such reels have a simple one-twist grooved arrangement, but on some such as the Zebco model pictured there is a lock to be disengaged. In the picture, the finger-operated locking button is just above the center of the handle.

The inner plastic dome is disengaged either by a half-turn, or simply lifted out by grasping its edges with the fingers. On some reels, a center screw holds the spool in place, in others it is kept in position by a retaining plate that must be taken off to free the spool. The cup can then be wiped clean and old lubricant removed from around the shaft, and fresh lubricant applied.

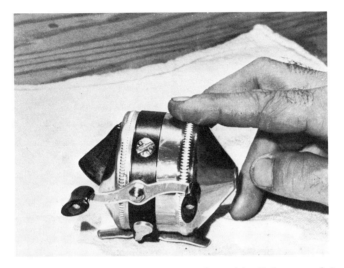

A typical closed-face spincast reel is this Zebco model. The cover plates on most such reels unlock with a half-turn for removal.

Gears and other mechanical components of spincast reels may be housed in a cylindrical compartment like this, accessible by removing the back cover with a half-turn and pull, or in a flattened semicircular frame with sideplates.

Removing the handle to free the gear shaft is the first operation in replacing the broken gear. Other components shown in this picture are the T-bar, which stretches across the center of the housing and is pressed by the thumb brake lever in the back cover to operate the line brake; the spool tension adjustment, under the forefinger at lower left; and the line release lever at left center outside the housing.

Removing the back plate gives access to the mechanism. Shown in the photo is the retaining catch, at top left, which holds the central T-bar in place; this bar transmits the action of the brake to the front of the reel. The handle shaft passes through the rectangular block at bottom left to operate the gears. When the handle is removed with pliers or a wrench, the shaft can be pushed forward a fraction of an inch to disengage the gears for removal, as demonstrated in the next photo. The thumbscrew on the outside of the frame at bottom left adjusts line tension.

The T-bar can be lifted out with the fingers, as shown. The main drive gear on the reel shown has been broken, probably due to the freezing of the shaft by the gummed lubricant that can be seen in the

After the T-bar is freed by pulling the slots of the line brake arms against the housing, it can be lifted out with the fingers. With the bar, the spool shaft and its tension spring are also removed.

Replacing the broken drive gear is accomplished by slipping the gear shaft out of the housing and inserting a new shaft-fitted gear. The broken gear, at left, was probably over-strained by old grease gummed up in the bottom of the compartment around the spool shaft. Cleaning and lubricating most reels of this kind seldom require complete stripping; a small kerosene-soaked brush is used to remove old lubricants.

This large brass circle with its inset O-ring is the line brake; one of the arms extending from the circle can be seen under the forefinger at left, the other arm is being used to hold the part. These arms pass through the body and are attached to the T-bar. The neoprene O-ring will sometimes pop out of its retaining grooves, and when this happens the entire assembly should be replaced.

bottom of the reel housing. The new gear, shown being inserted, is simply slipped into the housing; the nut holding the handle positions the gear automatically.

This large O-ring, which can be noted in earlier pictures in place around the spool, should be replaced at regular intervals. It is the line brake, and becomes rough and pitted with time. The rubber O-ring and its frame form a single unit and must be replaced as a unit. The ring itself should not be taken out of its frame and replaced separately; no matter how carefully the job is done, the O-ring will be twisted as it is

In this star-drag equipped spincast reel, a coin-slotted screw holds the spool retaining plate in place. The plate of this model is above the reel and contains the pickup pegs or fingers. One of these is at lower right, the other just over the handle at upper left.

being set in the frame and will pop out unexpectedly and jam the reel.

There are very slight internal differences between the Zebco spincast reel in the preceding sequence of pictures and the Model One illustrated; the Model One has a star drag and the spool is held in place by a screw instead of a retaining plate, as shown in the second photo. The spool-retaining screw is slotted and can be removed with a dime for a screwdriver if the spool is changed in the field. The pickup fingers are on a plate above the spool, and show clearly in the picture; if the top of the reel is considered 12:00 o'clock, the fingers are at 4:00 and 10:00 o'clock.

After the top plate and spool have been taken out, the bottom plate can be lifted out by prying it up gently with a screwdriver, as the

Under the spool are the drag washers, already removed and lying at left; between them is the retaining washer that holds them in position. The nylon buttons on either side of the spool shaft are activated by the drag handle to adjust pressure on the washers. A screwdriver is being used to lift out the back plate.

picture shows. Then, the spool cup can be serviced as described earlier.

The chief difference in the mechanism of this model from the reel shown previously is the crossed-axis gearing. It can be removed for cleaning or replacement by taking out the six Phillips screws that hold the shaft housings. The arced T-bar must be disengaged from the slots in the arms that connect it to the brake ring in the front section of the reel before it can be lifted out with the fingers. To disengage the T-bar, pull one arm at a time against the frame with the tip of a screwdriver.

These two Zebco spincast reels can be considered typical of all spincast reels in their basic features, and on opening any other make or model reel of this type you will find one of these two basic methods of gearing and other controls used.

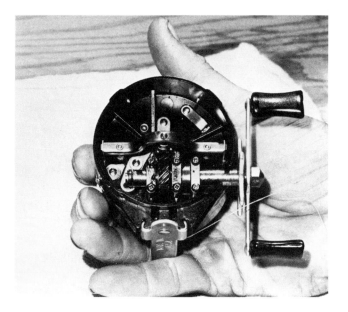

*A crossed-axis gearing is used in this reel. It is disassem-
bled by removing the Phillips-head screws at the top of the
handle shaft housing. The T-bar, arced in this mechanism,
performs the same function as the straight bar in the reel in
the previous sequence of pictures, and the remaining components are also similar to or identical with those of the
smaller reel.*

In their gearing, Shakespeare's spincast reels and the spincast reels
by some other makers are more like the open-face spinning reels
illustrated earlier. The star drag washers in these reels will be found in
the housing between handle and sideplate.

One component needing regular attention is the inner plastic dome
that guides the line to the pickup pins. Constant flexing of this part
causes it to break free from its retaining plate, and when this happens it
should be removed, dome and plastic cleaned, and the dome reglued
into place with epoxy.

A problem common to spincast reels with flexible plastic domes or cones is breaking of the glue bond that holds them to their supporting plates. Unlike O-rings, the domes can be quickly and easily reglued with epoxy.

Spincast reels are generally lighter in weight than their open-face cousins, and this lightness is achieved by a more extensive use of plastic components, such as frames, and by refining the gears to the safest possible minimum size and strength for the line loading recommended by their manufacturers. This is not to imply that spincast reels are fragile, but they are much more finely tuned than open-face reels, and any finely tuned mechanism calls for regular maintenance. A heavy-duty Diesel truck is more rugged and will carry heavier loads than will a racing car; the truck will do this with a minimum of servicing, while the racing car must be serviced before each race.

Freshwater spincast reels should never be loaded with monofilament heavier than that recommended by their manufacturer. Depending on make and model, these reels are generally recommended for use with lines on no more than a 2-pound test range, 6- to 8-pound or 8- to 10-pound or 10- to 12-pound test. Even though today's mono lines are smaller in diameter per pound of test than were those of a few years ago, the maker's recommendation should always be followed when changing the line on a spincast reel's spool.

There are, of course, heavy-duty closed-face reels designed for surf and offshore fishing, and these are made to handle mono up to 30- and 40-pound test. The only difference you will find when stripping these bigger reels is a difference in the size of their components; their functioning and construction are virtually identical with the lighter freshwater reels.

Baitcasting Reels

From the day when George Snyder assembled the first multiplying reel in the early 1800s until the present, the revolving-spool reel favored for casting plugs, spinners, and baits designed to attract such big fish as black bass, walleye, and muskellunge has undergone a lot of changes.

By the 1850s, baitcasting reels were being assembled with screws instead of brads or rivets, and within a very short time jeweled bearings came to replace metal-to-metal sockets, and sturdier gears and pinions machined specifically for fishing reels replaced clock parts. The next big step forward was development of the level-wind mechanism that deposited line evenly on the reel spool during a retrieve. Slower in coming were the free-spool mechanism that allowed the spool to revolve on a cast without dragging the deadweight of the handle; the centrifugal brake that prevented the spool from overrunning and creating a backlash; and, finally, the miniaturization of the star drag that made possible the use of lighter lines, and consequently a more varied selection of lures.

Perhaps these developments would have been even slower if the instant popularity of spinning reels after World War II hadn't cut deeply into baitcasting reel sales. Designers went back to their drawing boards to work out new baitcasting reels that could compete in ease of use and versatility with the spinning reel, which was winning new fishermen because no real practice was necessary to make long casts with it. At the same time, war technology in metals and plastics had created new materials that made more versatile baitcasting reels possible. By the late 1960s, they had regained lost ground and by the mid-1970s were being used to about the same degree as was spinning tackle.

There are a lot of good baitcasting reels around that date back to the preinnovative days of the 1950s and early 1960s, many still in excellent condition, and perfectly well suited for still-fishing and light trolling. These reels are also well suited for use by youngsters who like to toss a blob of worms or a minnow while the adults are plugging or flycasting, and there are also a lot of mature anglers who enjoy letting a worm or minnow work for them.

Most of these old-style reels are neglected because they've gotten corroded and the grease in their gears has frozen due to lack of use. A lot of tackle-tinkerers hesitate to take on the job of cleaning them up; they feel that because the reels are old-fashioned, they'll present unusual service problems. Actually, the reverse is true—these old jobs are much simpler than newer baitcasting reels with their multiple features.

Most of these old reels have a spool tension adjustment, a level-wind device, and a click—and not much else. Stripping one of them is a good way to learn the basics of baitcasting reel construction without having a lot of extra gears and rachets cluttering up the scene. Let's strip an old-timer, made by Bronson in the late 1940s, and in its day a very advanced reel.

As with any baitcasting reel, the first step in stripping is to take off the handle by removing the retaining nut that secures it, using a small wrench. After taking off the sapphire-jeweled spool bearings and spool cap, the sideplate screws are removed.

A single gear train serves the reel, which is typical of most baitcasting reels of its time. The gear is attached directly to the shaft of the handle; its outer ring of teeth engage the small gear in the center of the plate, which is keyed to the axle of the spool, and the small subsidiary teeth atop the main gear mesh with the gear on the frame that drives the level-wind worm. Dirt and hardened grease indicate that the reel is badly in need of cleaning.

Slipping out the spool gives access to the left sideplate, which is permanently attached to the frame. The pawl is removed by taking out a screw from the line guide support; above it, the worm drive gear can

Taking off the sapphire spool bearings at each end of this fine old Bronson reel is a finger job; these also double as oil cups. The next step is to remove the pillar screws.

As this photo of its very dirty innards shows, a single rim-toothed gear train serves the entire reel. The large ring gear meshes with a pinion keyed to the spool axle and the smaller ring gear meshes with the pinion on the frame to operate the level-wind's worm gear.

First step in stripping any level-wind mechanism on any reel is removing the pawl that rides the worm gear's slots. There has been no significant change in level-wind mechanisms since this device was invented.

be seen. The worm is slipped out of its housing after the pawl has been removed.

That's all there is to it—removing one nut, three screws, and two cover caps from the sideplates disassembles the reel completely. Its components, all twelve of them, are interesting to compare with a picture you'll encounter later of the components of a modern baitcasting reel. All the service and lubrication points of the stripped reel are readily apparent, and reassembly is as simple a job as was the stripping.

When you begin to strip a modern reel, with its many features, keep in mind the precaution advised earlier in this chapter: set aside an area next to that where you're working in which each part removed from the reel can be put in a line, so that when you begin to reassemble the reel you will know the sequence in which each component goes on the frame. It takes no time or effort to arrange the parts this way, and is very good insurance against mistakes.

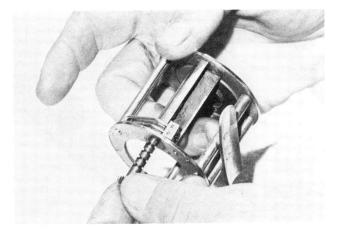

After removing the pawl, the worm gear is pulled from its housing.

Twelve parts plus two not removed from the reel make up the entire components list of this old-timer. Most of the parts are readily recognizable. The right sideplate is just above the spool, the handle is flanked by the spool bearings and handle nut, pillar screws are below the handle, the pawl and its retaining plate below the worm, the frame is at upper right. Remaining on the frame are the pawl housing and click mechanism. The safety pin? Keep one handy for pulling out that loose tag end of line that always catches between spool and frame when a line-loaded spool is being removed.

Modern baitcasting reels of the latest design generally share the same features, and because of the limitations of design and construction already noted, all will be very similar in the number and placement of components. The most popular reels in the full-function category are Garcia's Ambassadeur, Daiwa's Millionaire, Heddon's Mark 3200, Quick's 700 and 800 Champion series, and Shakespeare's Model 1975. All of these are excellent reels, all have the same features in slightly different form, all are within about the same price bracket, and choosing between them becomes a matter of brand loyalty and individual preference.

Features on all these reels are ball-bearing spool axles, level wind, free spool, centrifugal brake (automatic thumbing), spool brake, spool tension adjustment, spool designed for use with mono, and star drag. All are available in several models. The differences you'll find between these reels are such minor things as positioning of controls, use of an eyed instead of a slotted line guide, one disc more or less in the star drag, and exterior finish. The procedure followed in stripping them is essentially the same, as are the points that need lubrication, cleaning, or other maintenance.

Using the Garcia Ambassadeur as a typical reel of this category, stripping begins by removing the handle locknut and the antislip washer below the nut. The handle-retaining screw comes out next, and the handle is lifted off its shaft. This allows the star drag wheel to be removed by unscrewing it from its shaft. The spool bearing cover can be removed with the fingers, since it must often be taken off in the field to oil the bearing.

Removal of the right sideplate begins by taking out the pillar screws, which are both knurled for finger removal and slotted in case a screwdriver is required to loosen them. The sideplate is lifted off, exposing the end of the spool and the centrifugal brake. This brake is often called an automatic thumbing device, and the reel's maker provides two sets of weights that can be changed to compensate for differences in line size. The weights move back and forth on the bar that goes through the spool axle at right angles.

Before doing anything else, take the ball bearing out of the sideplate. It's easier to remove them at this point than earlier, when the bearings are still supporting the spool axle. Next, remove the spool,

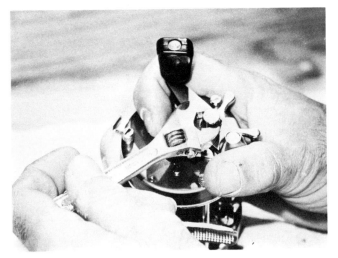

Stripping the Garcia Ambassadeur reel begins with removal of the handle nut and a spring-tension lock washer beneath it.

When the retaining screw under the nut is removed, the handle can be lifted off.

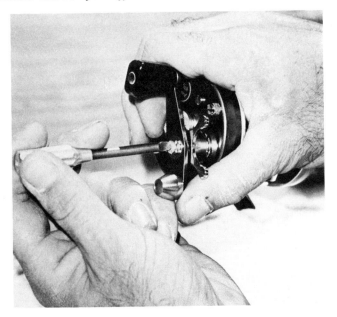

To remove it, turn the star drag control counterclockwise.

The spool bearing covers are removed with the fingers.

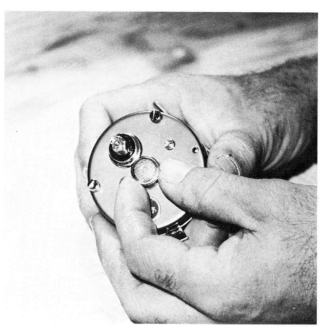

Although the pillar screws are slotted, removing them is usually done with the fingers also.

Crossing the axle in the end plate of the spool is the centrifugal brake, often called an "automatic thumb." The small weights at each end of its shaft are changed to compensate for differences in lines and lure weight. The right sideplate below the frame contains the brake and star drag mechanism as well as the main gear; these are now hidden by the inner cover plate.

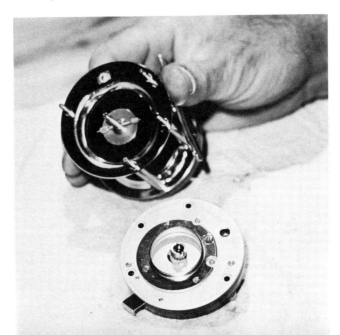

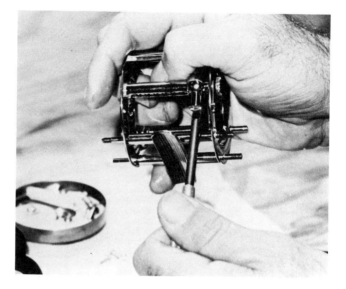

To remove the level-wind's worm gear, the pawl must be taken out.

A lift-out latch on the frame releases the level-wind worm.

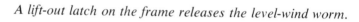

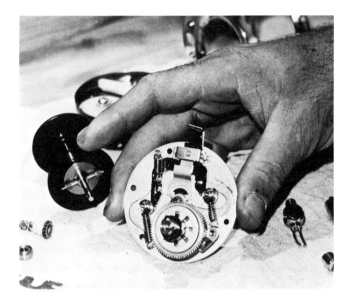

Two screws on the outer face of the right sideplate are taken out to separate the inner cover from the outside recessed plate. On the cover are mounted the main gears, star drag washers, and the thumb brake.

which is simply lifted out of the frame. Then take off the left-hand sideplate, which contains the click and antireverse mechanism. Complete stripping of the frame by taking off the level-wind gear. First, unscrew the pawl, as shown, and shake it out of its housing. A latch on the frame must be opened to release the level-wind worm gear; after the latch has been pulled open, the worm gear can be taken from its housing.

On the back of the right sideplate cover, which is separated from the plate by removing two screws on the outside of the plate, you will find the thumb brake with its yoke and two tension springs, the main drive gear, and the star drag mechanism, which is at the bottom of the plate as pictured. In the next photo, the main gear is shown in profile with the star drag washers separated on their shaft at the left of the gear. These are slipped off the shaft for cleaning or replacement.

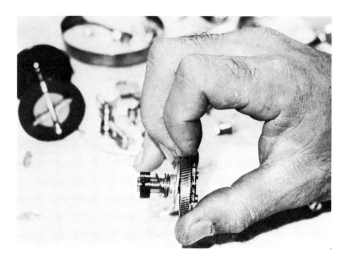

Here the star drag washers are shown in profile on their shaft. The wide fiber washer must be unscrewed, the others then lift off the shaft.

Finally, not in the sequence of removal as I've advised, but grouped for photographic reasons, are the reel's components, more than seventy-five of them, including the tensioning springs and others that should only be removed if replacement is necessary.

In reassembling the Ambassadeur reel, there is only one point at which you're likely to encounter a problem—in joining the right side-plate and its inner plate. Before tightening the screw indicated by the screwdriver and its companion directly below it, the thumb brake lever must be depressed to engage its yoke. The best position to hold the work is shown in the next photo, horizontal, with a forefinger "feeling" for the engagement point while the screwdriver is held ready to apply the final two or three turns. There will be a faint but audible click when the brake lever has been depressed the correct distance, and a small jar will be felt on the finger pressing the lever.

Finally, adjusting the bearing covers must be done with careful attention, since they also control the amount of free play the spool will

More than 75 components, including those not removed from their assemblies, go into a typical reel of this kind. The parts that might not be readily identifiable are the disassembled star drag in the center foreground and the right sideplate inner cover just above the washers; the star drag mechanism is mounted on the shaft at the bottom of this cover plate. Compare this with the earlier picture showing components of the Bronson reel.

When reassembling the Ambassadeur reel, the screws holding the right sideplate inner cover should not be finally tightened until the thumb brake lever is depressed to move its pawl a fraction of an inch.

Hold the sideplate horizontally at the angle shown and slowly depress the brake lever until you hear a small click. The cover screws can then be fully tightened.

have. Center the spool by tightening each bearing cover in turn, then tighten the covers alternately by quarter-turns until you can move the spool only a hairsbreadth from side to side within the frame. Tightening the covers too much will impede the spool's spin and may cause it to freeze; tightening them too little will allow excess play that results in undue bearing wear.

As you can see from the photo, the Daiwa Millionaire is an almost identical twin to the Ambassadeur. Just how much of a twin it is will become more apparent as we look at its innards. First, the Daiwa reel uses an exterior lock washer on the handle nut instead of a tension washer under the nut, and the lock washer must be removed by taking

In place of a spring tension washer, the Daiwa Millionaire uses an external screw-down lock washer to keep the handle nut from slipping.

out its retaining screw and lifted off, as shown. The handle's locknut cannot be loosened until this washer is taken off.

From this point the stripping procedure is exactly the same as that used with the Ambassadeur. First the handle nut is taken off with a wrench, then the retaining screw removed and the handle lifted off. Pillar screws on the Daiwa are not slotted and can be removed with the fingers. When the sideplate is removed, you see the same centrifugal brake system that will be found on any reel of this type. The gearing and star drag mechanism of the Daiwa are just about the same assembly that you'll see in the Ambassadeur or a similar full-function reel. There would have been as little difference if the comparison had been

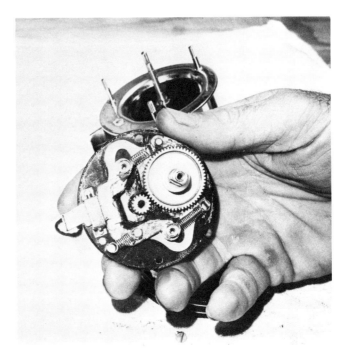

As noted earlier, function dictates form in fishing reels. On the inner cover of the sideplate are the main gear and star drag at upper right, the thumb brakes and yokes at left center. From this point on, you could follow the sequence for the Ambassadeur to strip the Daiwa and several other multifunction baitcasting reels.

made with a reel of another make. Incidentally, the Ambassadeur is the only reel of this type in which you must feel for a matchup when reassembling the cover plate and sideplate; in other reels they can be joined without jiggling the thumb brake lever.

As you can see by now, the differences between reels of the same type are merely superficial variations. Inside, you'll find much the same components assembled in much the same way. You'll also find the same points that need regular attention, chiefly cleaning and lubrication. These are the spool bearings, which can be lubricated simply by removing the cover plates, and any inner parts where there is metal-to-metal contact.

Don't be buffaloed by fear, then, when you have an old or new baitcasting reel that needs to be stripped for cleaning or repairs. Just grit your teeth and go ahead. You won't make any mistakes that can't be corrected.

Deep-sea Reels

Big, beefy reels designed to handle a plunging marlin, sailfish, tuna, or other denizens of the deep came late to the angling scene. It was not until the early twentieth century that rod and reel angling in offshore waters began to develop as a major aspect of sport fishing.

Early saltwater reels were little more than enlarged versions of a freshwater baitcasting reel. Basically, they still are, but these early deep-sea reels lacked such features as free spooling and star drags, and deep-sea fishing was a pastime that resulted in bloody, often broken, fingers. In the first deep-sea reels, the angler used his fingers as a brake, pressing on a flap of thick leather attached to a back reel pillar to keep the fast-running line from burning and cutting his hand. When he had to slow down the run of a taking fish, he was forced to try to time his grabs at the reel handle to coincide with the few occasional seconds when the handle slowed down. For every deep-sea fisherman who got a finger burned by a fast-running line, ten got their knuckles bruised and skinned by mistiming their grabs at the reel handle. Not for nothing were those first deep-sea reels nicknamed ''knuckle-busters.''

Free-spool reels came to deep-sea fishing long before the average reel used in freshwater angling had this feature; the same thing is true of the star drag. Today's saltwater reels are much lighter and more versatile than those of earlier days; like freshwater tackle, they have benefited from modern developments in metallurgy and plastics. Today's deep-sea reel will have such features as free spool, star drag, antibacklash, and self-closing oil ports. The reels designed for lighter work than handling thousand-pound fish, those used in pier fishing and close inshore trolling and surfcasting, are often designed so that they can be field-stripped by taking out a few thumbscrews, an especially valuable feature when reels are used on sandy beaches where they may be dropped.

A saltwater reel's chief point of vulnerability has already been noted: the minute gap between spool and cover plate into which salt spray from a line running out fast or being reeled in fast will penetrate. Although noncorrosive materials are used wherever possible in deep-sea reels, salt is a great destroyer of metal surfaces. A saltwater reel should not only be stripped, cleaned, and oiled after a day's fishing, but the spool should be emptied and cleaned. Penn Fishing Tackle Company, which manufactures ocean fishing reels up to size 16/0, has a word of advice in its instruction books that is worth repeating here: "One drop of oil in the right place is worth more than two drops alongside." That modest understatement should be kept in mind not only when lubricating a saltwater reel, but any fishing reel.

Basically, a deep-sea reel is a scaled-up baitcasting reel with its components enlarged proportionately to its size. Although level-wind devices are included on the smaller saltwater reels used in surf and pier fishing and close-in offshore fishing, they're seldom found on the really big fellows that go out to deep water in search of the huge, tough battlers such as marlin. You will find that the same procedures used in stripping baitcasting reels apply to their bigger brothers.

There's one essential tool needed in stripping such reels as the Penn Senator 9/0 illustrated, and that's the serrated-jaw wrench shown in the foreground between the reel and the end wrench. You can use pliers to take the handle nut off, but you'll damage it if you do, so nurture this piece of free equipment furnished by the manufacturers when you buy a reel of this size.

Before applying the wrench to the handle nut, be sure to remove the locking screw that is nestled in one of the nut's grooves, as shown. Then the wrench frees the handle nut, just as in smaller reels, and a screwdriver is used to take out the pillar screws.

Sideplate, inner coverplate, and spool come out as a unit. Removing the plate also releases the lugs to which the fighting harness is buckled at the top of the reel and the rod clamps at its bottom.

Now the spool and sideplate can be slipped apart. The inner cover at the top of the sideplate holds the star drag mechanism—just like the

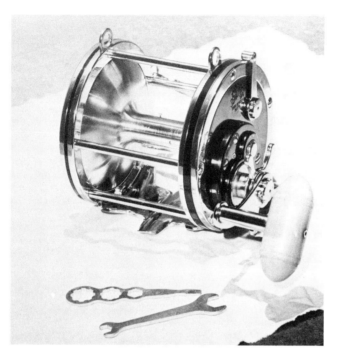

The chief difference between freshwater baitcasting reels and ocean reels with revolving-spool construction, such as this 9/0 Penn Senator, is one of size.

A lock-screw prevents shifting of the handle nut.

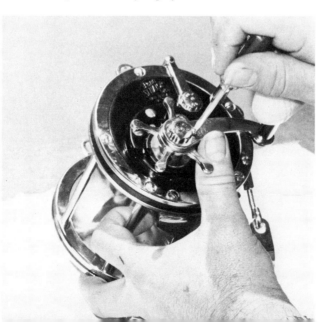

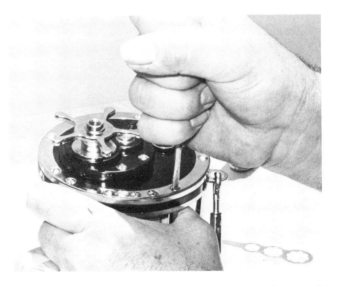

Stripping procedure is basically the same as that used in disassembling a small baitcasting reel. Pillar screws are removed.

Ocean reels are really simpler than multifunction freshwater baitcasting reels; the big saltwater jobs don't have centrifugal brakes, level-wind, thumb brakes and similar mechanisms. Under the cover plate shown, the star drag and gearing of this reel are like those on smaller reels except for the size of the components.

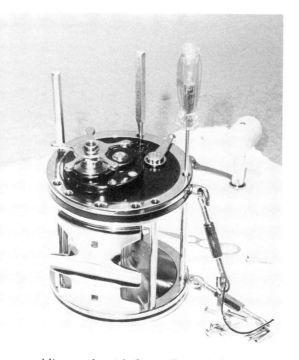

When reassembling reels with free pillars, driftpins should be used to align the sideplates. Punches such as those pictured, small screwdrivers, ice picks, all make effective driftpins. Be sure the lugs for the harness and auxiliary rod clamp are in their proper slots.

star drag on a small baitcasting reel, except that the washers are bigger. Points to check for maintenance are the ends of the spool axle and the bearings; remove the old lubricant by wiping, then washing the area with a kerosene-soaked brush and wiping off the thin residue that will remain. Deep-sea reels are usually fitted with self-closing oiling ports and can be lubricated without having to be stripped. This is both good and bad. It's good because it encourages regular lubrication, but bad because it discourages stripping the reel and can result in a buildup of old, hardened grease.

143

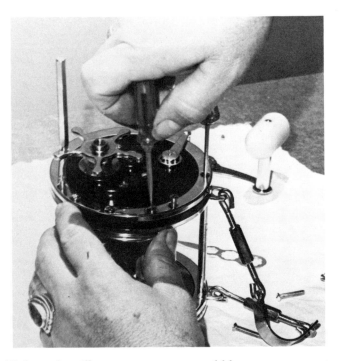

Tighten the pillar screws as you would lugs on an automobile wheel: alternately, crisscrossing the axis of the reel.

Always use driftpins when reassembling such a big reel. If you don't have any thin-nosed punches like those being used in the picture for driftpins, use a tiny screwdriver or two, an old icepick, or even nails of a suitable diameter. You need three driftpins to line up the pillars and sideplate. And be sure to replace both harness lugs and clamp lugs in their proper places before starting the screws.

Replace the screws beginning at the foot, and tighten them as a careful mechanic tightens the lugs on an automobile wheel—working across the reel in a series of Xs instead of going around its rim in a circle.

One final suggestion on general reel maintenance and repairs: When you buy a new reel, be sure and keep the instruction book instead of glancing at it and discarding it. If you buy a used reel, write the manufacturer's Customer Service Department, giving the reel's model, and ask for a new booklet. And, if you sell a reel to a friend, remember to pass the instruction booklet along to him. Sooner or later he'll thank you for your thoughtfulness.

4

LINES AND LEADERS

Although taking care of fishing lines isn't the constant chore it used to be in the days of enameled silk fly lines, braided silk casting lines, and linen cuttyhunk deep-sea lines, there are still some things you should do to keep your lines in tip-top shape. And there are also some tricks you can use to get extra life out of a line that you might think was ruined.

Development of new kinds of fishing lines has paralleled that of the creation of new kinds of rods and reels. The matched tackle concept, which until the middle 1960s was confined to fly-fishing, has now become commonplace. Anglers using spinning and baitcasting tackle, who once grinned smugly to themselves when they watched the effort spent by fly-fishermen to achieve a perfect relationship between rod, line, and reel, now spend about the same amount of time fly-fishermen do in working out the tackle components that will give them the best results in their spin-fishing or baitcasting.

Part of the reason for this changed attitude toward balanced tackle is the result of continuing improvements in the tackle itself, but a lot of it is due to the better understanding anglers have of their tackle. Changed fishing conditions also play an important part in our approach to the sport itself. It hasn't been too many years since a fisherman willing to get up early and drive to the end of a rugged road and then hike for an hour or two could find seldom-visited waters inhabited by fish that weren't tackle-shy. Now, greater pressure on more readily accessible streams and lakes, including the tremendous number of new fish-stocked artificial impoundments, has conditioned fish to be much more wary. Even fish fresh from the hatchery ponds soon learn to avoid lures offered with coarse terminal tackle.

When man first began to fish with a line, his coarse lines of braided bark fibers or thin vines didn't spook the fish because they hadn't learned to suspect a gobbet of food offered them with a line attached to it might be dangerous to their health. It didn't take them long to get the idea, though, and fishing history since then has been a contest of reason against instinct as anglers try to keep refining terminal tackle to make it inconspicuous and also keep creating new lures to attract fish grown wary of familiar ones.

History doesn't record all the stages of evolution through which fishing lines have passed, but horsehair was a favorite material used in braided lines as well as for leader material in the early days of angling, and undoubtedly every fiber produced by spinning mills was used experimentally in fishing lines.

Silk cloth came to the Western world from the Far East long before someone thought of using its fine supple threads for fishing lines. Development of the first braided silk lines is credited to Frederic Halford, a British angler of the early 1800s. Halford's first lines were soft, untreated, and required a lot of false casting to dry them between casts so they wouldn't cling to the rod when casting began and would float briefly after they landed on the water. By the 1870s, though, the use of linseed oil-impregnated silk lines was commonplace, and the discovery of a way to coat the sticky oil-soaked lines with a flexible varnishlike outer finish soon followed.

Braided silk baitcasting lines were first made in the United States by a Connecticut angler, Elisha Martin, in the mid-1880s. Martin's lines were stiff and coarse, but they did not rot out as quickly as had the cable-laid lines that were the only kind available earlier. These first braided casting lines, like Halford's original fly lines, were available in only one diameter or test. In the late 1880s, the process of braiding silk lines around a stranded core of fine silk floss was evolved, and both fly and baitcasting lines entered what might be called the modern era.

When deep-sea fishing became popular at the turn of the century, neither silk nor cotton proved satisfactory for lines. A line of soft silk, under the strain of playing heavy ocean fish, would dig into the layers already on the reel's spool and form snarls that became knots when the line was next paid out, and these knots stopped the spool abruptly, usually breaking the line. Cotton was unpredictable in strength, the equipment then in use could not produce lines that were uniform or free from bulges and thin spots. Linen proved the answer, and in the 1890s members of an angling club on Cuttyhunk Island, off the Massachusetts coast, developed superior deep-sea lines of linen. While not all the linen lines that began to be manufactured in that era were entitled to bear the name, "Cuttyhunk" soon passed into the language and became a generic term describing all cable-laid linen lines.

A distinction needs to be made between the two types of lines, braided and cable-laid. Braiding of lines began with horsehair and wound up with silk, later with synthetic fibers known by a number of trademarked names, the best-known being nylon and Dacron. Linen is not suitable for braiding because it tends to shear where the braided fibers cross. Cable-laid is a term deriving from the days when ship's cordage was produced by twisting fibers into cords, the cords into ropes, the ropes into cables, on a long rope walk. Due to their construction, cable-laid lines tend to twist in use; with the advent of synthetic fibers that can be braided without shearing and that can also be precisely controlled to give any desired stretchiness or springiness and produced from filaments of a controlled diameter, natural fibers have just about vanished from the angling scene.

Early synthetic lines had problems, the biggest of which, their tendency to stretch under strain, was the underlying cause of most others. Braided nylon baitcasting and ocean fishing lines were so springy that in long-line fishing it was hard to set hooks securely. Fly lines stretched under their coatings, causing the coating to crack and peel off. The hot-stretch finishing process that was developed in the mid-1950s proved the answer to most synthetic line problems, and today's synthetic fibers produce lines better in all respects than the old natural-fiber lines.

One of the advantages of modern synthetic-fiber lines is that they don't need the constant care natural fiber lines required. It's a good idea, though no longer a real necessity, to wash saltwater lines if they're going to be unused for a while. However, it's not necessary to put fly and baitcasting lines on drying frames at the end of a day's fishing, as was once the case. All lines do need occasional attention, though, if you're going to get out of them the full service life they can give you.

Care Required by All Lines

No matter whether you fish with fly, spinning, baitcasting, or deep-sea tackle, your lines will get dirty. Though lines used in warm water need cleaning more often than do those used in mountain streams or lakes, all living water contains some algae, and this will collect on every kind of fishing line, including monofilament. When a line gets caught in underwater weeds, it must be dragged through them, picking up some of the secretions from the vegetation itself as well as from any algae or slime that may be caught on it. These deposits will be invisible or next to invisible, but they're there, and on them collect microscopic particles of the organic matter that's suspended in all water.

Rarely will these deposits react harmfully on a line's finish, but they do tend to attract grit and dirt particles. Then, especially if your line is used for bottom fishing, or if you drop some of its coils on the sandy shore from which you're fishing, abrasive bits of matter will be picked up by the line. If the line isn't cleaned, these rough spots will eventually score your rod guides and some of them will work into the line itself to weaken it, or in the case of mono, will cause rough areas that score guides.

Occasional wiping of the portion of your lines most often in the water is a good idea. Use a soft nonabrasive material, a clean cloth or a chamois, or one of the soft synthetic sponges used in car washing and photo labs. I use a kind of spongy towel that is made from some sort of foamed plastic, and sold in most supermarkets for less than $1 a roll. The rolls are about the size of paper towel rolls, and the material lasts and lasts. One roll should be a lifetime supply for fishing use.

Unless you habitually fish in warm, mossy waters loaded with algae, your lines will need to be cleaned only once or twice a year. At the end of the season, though, they should be wiped clean while you're storing your tackle away. While wiping, check braided lines for frayed spots and mono for roughened areas. Wire lines, both stranded and solid, should be given the same treatment and inspected for kinks that are potential trouble spots. This checkup may give you a hint that you've got a guide problem on one of your rods, since a rough, scored guide will leave an obvious and potentially troublesome sign on a line.

All braided lines can be freed from rough or frayed spots, and fly lines can be cleared of places where bad cracks occur in their finish by cutting out the trouble area and splicing the line. We'll get to this later on.

Fly Lines

Many fly lines are sold with a small quantity of cleaning compound recommended by the manufacturer, and since fly lines cost much more than any other kind to replace, it's good sense to follow their maker's recommendations in cleaning them. It's also good practice to transfer your lines for off-season storage to a reel that has a larger diameter than a fishing reel. Although a modern fly line won't be damaged by being left on its reel the year around, unless it's stored in absolutely ideal conditions it will tend to settle into tight coils that must be worked out by stretching the line when it's used again.

Storage reels aren't as common as they used to be, when it was almost mandatory that silk lines be taken off the fly reel at the end of the day and coiled loosely or placed on a storage reel to dry out overnight. And I've never known a fly-fisherman yet who owned only one line for each rod or reel he had. Most of them are like me and have three times as many fly lines as they can use regularly; for these spare lines, big-reel storage is still an important maintenance factor.

The best storage reels I own were designed and made by Charlie Kewell, who had a three-quarter century career of innovative angling in his small ship just at the edge of San Francisco's Skid Row. If you have a woodworking hobbyist friend whose shop includes a lathe, you might persuade him to turn out some duplicates of the Kewell reels shown in the picture. Their outside diameter is 8¼ inches, the groove

Storage reels such as these keep fly lines in better condition than they'll be if left on a small-diameter fly reel spool during the off-season.

that accommodates the line is 1 inch wide and ¾ inch deep. They're made from glued-up scraps of hardwoods and varnished.

With simple tools you can make a half-dozen storage reels in a half hour out of a plastic minnow bucket and some scraps of hardboard or plywood, though hardboard is preferable since it doesn't have any splinters to dig hands while line is being transferred to the reel.

Get a round plastic minnow bucket, stick a nail through it from the inside to mark the point where its bottom starts. Snap a rubber band around the bucket just above the nail to give you a true line, easily adjustable, for marking the bucket off in lengths of about 1 inch, as shown in the picture. Cut or saw along these lines to produce as many plastic circles as the number of reels you want to make. Use the circles to mark your hardboard rims; these will vary as the inner and outer diameters of the plastic circles change due to the bucket's tapering shape. You need two rims for each reel; the outer diameter of the rims should be about ¾ inch larger than the outer diameter of the plastic circle that will form the inside of your reel.

Using a saber saw or a woodworker's coping saw, fretsaw, or keyhole handsaw, cut the circles out of the hardboard. Glue the plastic

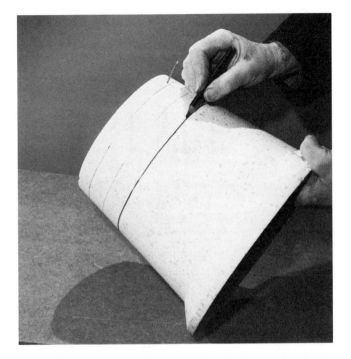

To make line storage reels, cut a plastic minnow bucket into slices. Each slice makes one reel.

Knife and saw are equally efficient when cutting the bucket into loops.

Use the loops to mark hardboard rims for the reels. Each loop will have a slightly different diameter due to the bucket's taper.

A saber saw, coping saw, or keyhole saw can be used to cut the rims.

circles cut from the minnow bucket to the hardboard circles. Be sure to test any adhesive you use on a scrap of the plastic from the bucket, for some of the synthetic adhesives will dissolve some types of foamed plastic materials. There's no way for you to know in advance which of the adhesives available will be compatible with the formulation of the minnow bucket's plastic, so test them out. Then, glue a plastic circle inside each pair of hardboard rims. When the glue sets up, you'll have line storage reels like the one illustrated—not candidates for exhibiting in a craft show, but adequate for the job they're intended to do.

You should know a little about fly line history should you decide to take on the job of restoring or renovating a line that's been damaged.

While silk fly lines were pioneered by Frederic Halford in England, it was the late Leon P. Martuch in the United States who pioneered the modern fly line and contributed the most to the versatile array of lines fly-fishermen enjoy using today. Halford developed the art of building lines of different weights, diameters, and tapers for different rods and styles of fishing; Martuch adapted modern synthetic fibers to the creation of lines that needed no oily dressing to make them float, no slimy gunk or frangible metal cores to make them sink fast.

In the late 1940s, Martuch created two new kinds of fly lines. One, called the "Air-Cel," had an inner core of a flexible plastic that was aerated to trap masses of almost microscopically tiny bubbles. This line floated without any of the oil-based dressings formerly needed to achieve a floating line for dry-fly fishing. Martuch engineered the second line with a core that contained graphitic particles that gave it a lesser specific gravity than water, which caused it to sink rapidly. This line he named the "Wet-Cel." Martuch formed a firm, Scientific Anglers, which today, as part of the 3M industrial complex, is still making these lines.

Other manufacturers soon began producing lines based on Martuch's discoveries. Some used aerated plastic coatings in their floating lines, and weighted coatings in their sinking lines, but the end results were the same. Outer coatings of tough plastic, much less susceptible to damage than the earlier enameled coatings, also came into use.

In spite of the toughness of today's fly lines, they can still be damaged when ground by a careless foot into hard rocks or gritty sand; they can still be crushed in a car door or caught in a crevice between a

Your finished reel should look like this, nothing fancy, but a very efficient and inexpensive storage reel.

couple of razor-sharp rocks. Even though the damage to the line's finish is minimal, it will soon be increased by friction of the line passing through the guides, or by its flexing during casting. Small flaws grow larger and soon the line becomes useless.

Small frayed or marred spots can be repaired several ways. If the crack or break is very tiny, so small that flexing of the line will not crack a protective coating, a small dab of epoxy can be worked into the break to seal it. Epoxy is brittle when dry, and any crack that is sizable should be mended with a permanently flexible adhesive material. Pliobond attacks the finish of some fly lines, but on others it can be worked into cracks or frayed spots to protect them and keep them from enlarging. Lines that are vulnerable to being attacked by Pliobond are usually immune to either the Dow-Corning or General Electric silicone adhesive—usually sold as a caulking material for bathroom or kitchen tile joints. Both these silicone preparations stay flexible when they have set up, and when set form slick, waterproof surfaces.

To make a repair using one of these materials, simply deposit a small blob of the adhesive on the frayed spot, then work it into the fibers of the line with your fingers, stroking the loose ends into the adhesive until the surface of the line is smoothly rounded. The only sign that such a repair has been made will be a light-colored spot on the line.

If a line has suffered extensive damage, it may be necessary to remove the marred portion and splice the line. Removing as much as 3 to 5 inches from a fly line will seldom affect its balance to your favorite rod. In fact, before the adoption of standards by the tackle industry, line diameters and weights often differed pretty widely from the data given on the label, and it was frequently necessary to shorten a line or to insert a piece of heavier line in its belly to get a good balance to a rod. Splicing may even help you to get the best match between line and rod. One of my own lines contains seven different diameters, involving a half-dozen splices, between the tip and the shooting backing.

Equipment needed for fly-line splicing includes a heavy needle set into some kind of handle such as a piece of dowel or a pin vise, fly-tying floss or thread, a tube of one of the cyanoacrylate monomer "miracle adhesives," and either a liquid finish such as fly-head cement or color preservative or one of the flexible adhesives mentioned earlier.

You will also need some kind of device to hold the line firmly. The rod-winding holder described and pictured in Chapter 2 can be adapted for use in either of two ways: by clipping the line to the rod-holding arms with clothespins, or by taking out the dowel that holds the spools of thread and slipping a loop of line through the holes it fits, using a short piece of dowel, a pencil stub, or a wooden kitchen match to hold the loop in place, as shown in the photo. Or, you can use a piece of plywood or hardboard from your scrap heap, and clip the line to it with clothespins as shown in the next picture.

You can tell quite readily which type of line you have to work with by cutting a slit in it about ½ inch from an end and inspecting it closely. One type has a braided core of Dacron or nylon and a plastic sheath that is either bubble-filled or weighted; the other has an inner core of

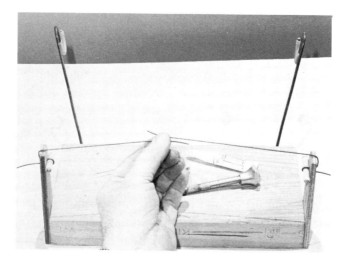

If you build a rod holder like the one pictured earlier, it can be used as a holder for lines being spliced as shown in this photo.

A piece of plywood to which the lines can be clipped with clothespins is as good as any other holder. You do need something to secure the lines when splicing, unless you have four hands.

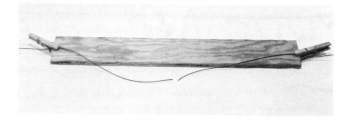

Form each of the frayed ends into a V that looks approxi-mately like these.

aerated or weighted plastic covered by a sheath of braided Dacron or nylon. To splice a line in the first type, remove the coating for about ⅜ to ½ inch from the ends; to splice a line in the second type, peel back the sheath for the same distance and remove a section of the core.

Fix the line in the holder to give you about 2 inches of working slack; an overlap such as pictured in the illustration showing the rod winder being used will give you an idea. With the needle, fray the braided core of type-one line or the braided sheath of type-two line. Then, as the photo illustrates, form each of the frayed ends into a V shape.

Push the bottom points of the two Vs together so the ends of the line are butted up into contact with one another, and stroke the frayed fibers out to cover the section of line each bunch of fibers overlaps. Then wrap the overlapped area tightly with several widely spaced turns of thread, as shown. You don't need to worry about tying off this wrapping, or about it being neat; it will be covered up later. I've found that doubling the thread makes this wrap a lot easier. Now, hold the ends of the wrapping thread taut while you put a scanty drop of the adhesive on it as illustrated.

Caution: Do not touch the splice while this adhesive is wet. It will dry in about two to three minutes, penetrating through the fibers and working into the spot where the two ends of the line are butted together. The caution is given because these ''miracle adhesives'' stick

159

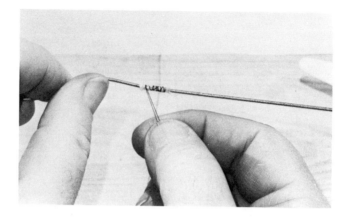

Push the ends of the lines together with the Vs at right angles to each other. The lines should be butted together where the frayed portion ends and the frayed portion of one line overlaps the solid portion of the other. Smooth the frayed fibers around the lines, and with rod or fly-tying thread make six or eight widely spaced turns around the overlapped lines. Don't bother to tie off the thread, just hold it as illustrated while applying the adhesive.

to human skin. Be patient. Don't try to squeeze the fibers together to get a better-looking splice. If you hesitate to use cyanoacrylate monomer adhesive, use Pliobond and let the splice set up for fifteen to thirty minutes. With Pliobond, you can safely touch the wet joint to make it smooth.

When the adhesive is dry, trim off the ends of the thread used to make the temporary wrap and cover the entire splice with a thread wrapping, just as you'd wrap a rod section. After pulling the wrapping thread or floss through and trimming it, give the wrapping a coating of preservative or rub it with Pliobond to form a smoothly tapered coating.

You need have no fear of a splice made this way parting, if you have followed the directions carefully. Before modern lines were

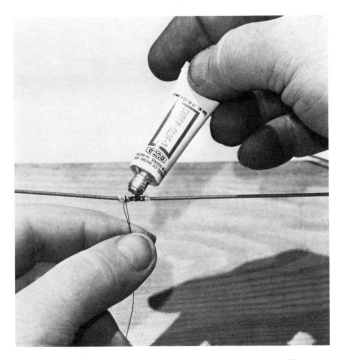

Put a scanty drop of cyanoacrylate monomer adhesive on the overlapped lines. See the text for details and precautions about using this adhesive.

developed, I spliced hundreds of lines in balancing tackle or for tournament casting, and have never had a properly made splice fail; in fact, the splice is stronger than the line. While I've made only forty or fifty splices in the new generation of fly lines, using either Pliobond or cyanoacrylate monomer glues, I've used these lines and tested the splices by pulling at them, and they've all held.

Braided Lines

Both baitcasting and saltwater fishing lines are generally braided of a synthetic fiber, usually Dacron or of some other polyester fiber. Cortland Line Company, for example, uses the trademarked name Micron for the synthetic fiber that goes into many of their lines. Except for the lead-cored lines used in deepwater trolling, most braided lines are coreless, and can be spliced quite readily in tests ranging from 20-pound test upward.

Almost all the synthetic fiber lines are highly water-resistant, and need not be spooled into a special reel to dry or washed after use in salt water. Many, if not most, synthetic fibers are prematurely aged by exposure to the ultraviolet rays of the sun. This means that you should not carry a reel loaded with such lines on the package shelf of your car, or on the car seat, where they will be bathed in direct sunlight for long periods of time. Prolong their useful life by carrying your line-filled reel in a case or a box or even a plain brown paper bag.

Splicing braided lines is done with a splicing needle similar to the lock-latchet needle used in crewel work or embroidery. The process is quick and simple. To make the following directions more easily understandable, let's call the lines to be spliced "A" and "B."

Insert the needle into line A about 3 to 4 inches from its end and run it through about 1 to 1½ inches of the center of the line, passing it to the outside about 2 inches from the end of the line, as shown in the first photo.

To splice a braided line with a splicing needle, slide the needle through the center of one line—let's call it A—about 3 to 4 inches from its end.

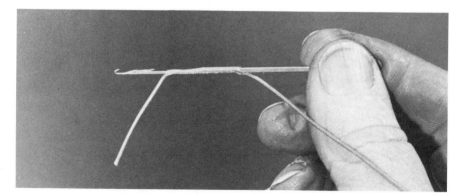

Make a flat loop in line B and insert it in the latchet end of the splicing needle; you will need 2½ to 3 inches of free end on line B, as the picture shows. Pull the doubled loop of line B through the center of line A. The gate or latchet at the end of the needle will close and allow the loop of line B to be pulled through without snagging.

Make a loop in the second line—B—about 3 to 4 inches from its end and catch line B in the splicing needle, as shown, by the center of the loop.

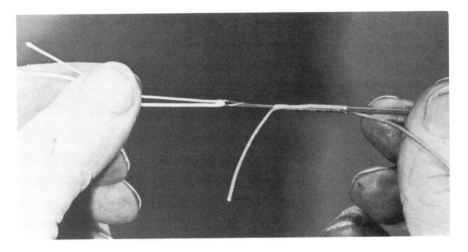

Pull the looped line—line B—through the center of line A; the latchet on the splicing needle closes to allow this to be done.

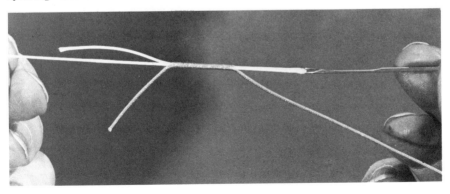

Now put the splicing needle through the center of line B, carrying it through the line for about 1 inch, just as you did with line A, and pull a loop of line A through the center of line B. The loop, of course, is made in the loose end of line A below the point where it passes through line B, as the picture illustrates.

Pull the loop of line A through the center of line B and disengage the needle. You now have about 1 inch of line A passing through the center of line B, and about 1 inch of line B passing through the center of line A, as shown.

Free the needle and push it through the center of line B beyond the point at which line B enters line A. Form a loop in the end of line A, grasp it with the needle, and pull it through the center of line B.

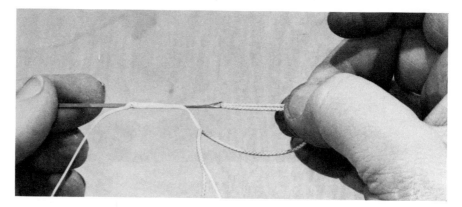

Holding both lines below the splice, pull them until line A meets line B where they pass through each other's center. Finally, trim off the loose ends of each line. To prevent excess wear or fraying, you can either wrap the ends of the splice with thread, or rub into them a bit of Pliobond or the silicone material mentioned earlier in this section.

You can use the splicing needle to make line-end loops by pulling a portion of line back through itself. If you splice a lead-cored line, you must remove the core from the portions of line that are to be pulled through the center of the other line. You can also use the splicing needle to insert the end of a fly line in a backing line, but it is not

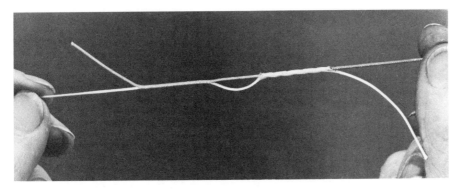

Your splice should now look like this. Pull the two lines together, line A traveling through the center of line B and vice versa.

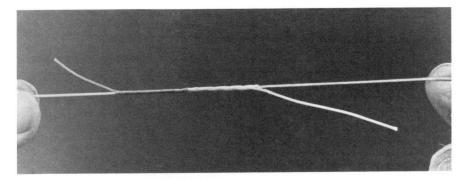

Now, your splice should look like this.

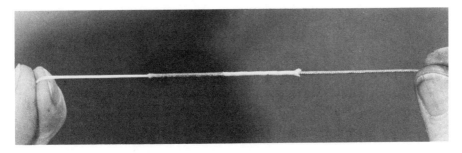

Trim off the loose ends to complete the splice. You can wrap the ends with thread to keep them from fraying, or by working Pliobond or silicone caulk into the ends and rolling them smooth between your fingers.

practical to make an interlocking splice such as the one illustrated, since the coating on most fly lines is not elastic enough to allow the needle to pass through its center. When pulling an end of fly line into a braided backing line, the splice should be coated with Pliobond and wrapped with thread.

Wire Lines and Leaders

Wire lines of stranded steel, solid steel or Monel, or some other alloy are used for deep trolling in big waters. Monel is preferred by many fishermen; it is an alloy of nickel, copper, and tin, and is more flexible than stainless steel, stronger and more kink-resistant than copper, and highly rust-resistant even in salt water. Stranded steel lines are often coated with vinyl or some other plastic to make them more resistant to rusting and easier to handle.

All wire lines occasionally throw a kink that must be removed and the line rejoined by splicing. The only alternative to a sleeved splice is a wrapped silver-soldered splice or a joint made by creating interlocked loops, as a swivel or snap is joined to a wire leader. Few anglers have the equipment or experience to handle silver soldering, and a loop splice is a clumsy affair at best in the middle of a metal line. However, a perfectly adequate loop splice can be made by using roundnose pliers, and the technique is the same as that used in forming loop eyes, which you will find pictured later on.

The easiest and most satisfactory way to splice either stranded or solid wire line, or to attach swivels or snaps to a wire leader, is to use a sleeve. This involves getting a pair of crimping pliers; there are pliers of this type made especially for fishing tackle, which cost about $4 to $5 a pair. Electrician's crimping pliers work just as well on all but the smallest sleeves.

To make a sleeved splice in either stranded or solid wire line, slip a sleeve of the proper size on one of the line ends and below it wrap the ends together three turns as shown in the first picture, bending the ends in over the center of the wrap, as shown in the picture.

Slide the sleeve over the wrap, pushing the ends of each wire through the sleeve and slowly pull the standing ends of the line in

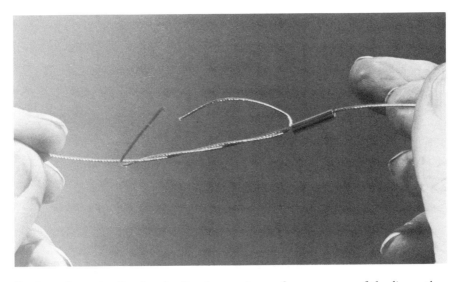

Begin a sleeved splice in wire line by putting a sleeve on one of the lines; then make three turns to join the lines and bend their ends over the wrapped portion.

Slide the sleeve over the crossed ends and the wrapped section as shown, then pull both lines until the wrap is covered by the sleeve.

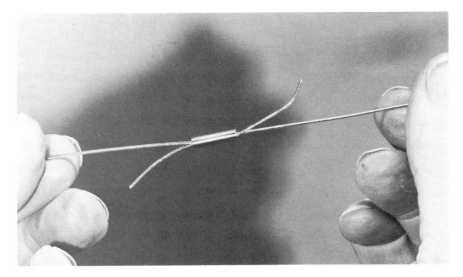

Crimp the sleeve at both ends and in the center.

opposite directions as shown, to tighten the wrap inside the sleeve. Crimp each end of the sleeve with the pliers, as illustrated, and trim off the loose ends to form a finished splice.

You can get splicing sleeves of several sizes, made of a number of different materials: brass, lead, stainless steel, or nylon. When choosing sleeves for your lines, though, remember that when ferrous and nonferrous metals remain in close contact in water—especially in salt water—both metals may corrode. When possible, use sleeves from the same type of metal from which the line is made.

Wire leaders, used by many freshwater fishermen after walleye, muskellunge, northern pike, and other sharp-toothed fish, can be joined together or can be fitted with new snaps or swivels or connectors by using sleeves. There are many saltwater species with teeth

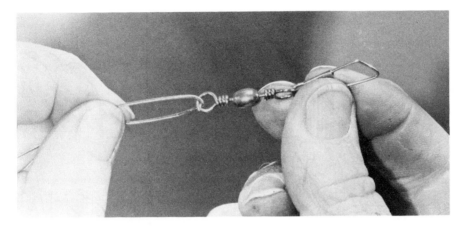

When replacing a snap or swivel on wire leader, thread on the swivel and pass the end of the leader twice through the eye of the swivel.

serrated along their entire length, and a wire leader or trace is a wise precaution when fishing offshore.

Replacing a swivel or snap on a wire leader is even simpler than splicing a line. First, pass the end of the wire through the eye of the

Wrap the end of the leader three times around the standing portion and bend the end back up toward the swivel.

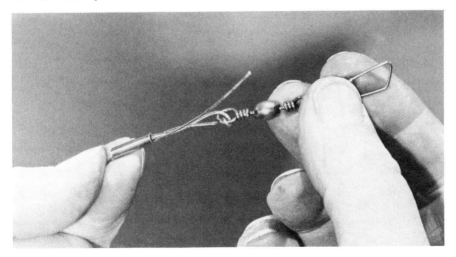

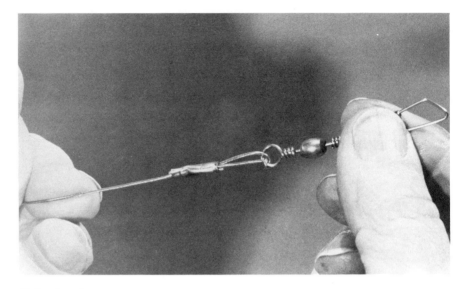

Slide the sleeve over the turns and bent-forward end, pull until the sleeve covers the turns. Crimp the sleeve, trim off the loose end to finish the operation.

swivel twice, as illustrated, leaving about 1 inch of spare line. Take three turns with the end of the line around its standing portion and bring the end back up and over the standing line and parallel to it. Slide the sleeve over the turns and pull gently but firmly on the swivel and standing line until the turns are compressed inside the sleeve. Then, crimp the sleeve, trim off the surplus end, and there's your swivel, attached by a neat loop.

Monofilament

Monofilament cannot be spliced in the true sense of the word. It is, as its name indicates, a solid filament without braid or twist, and can be joined together only with knots. Although there are nylon sleeves available to be used in forming loops and splices in mono, I frankly don't trust them. Put it down to blind prejudice, if you will, but I find it significant that no manufacturer of monofilament fishing lines and leaders makes or recommends these sleeves. I've never been tempted to experiment with them because I've learned to tie blindfolded or in the dusk and with wet, frozen fingers the three or four knots that will hold well in monofilament without reducing its strength.

The blood knot, sometimes called the barrel knot, is the best, easiest, and quickest way to splice two pieces of mono together, whether they are of the same or of different diameters. A properly tied blood knot will pass through guides without catching, and reduces the test strength of the mono by only 13 percent, while some highly thought of knots cut mono's rated test by as much as 60 percent. A lot of fishermen cuss the blood knot, but that's because they haven't learned the easy way to tie it without having to use three hands.

Here's how it's done. Hold the two pieces of mono to be joined between the thumb and forefinger of your right hand, as shown. You'll

Start a blood or barrel knot by holding between your right thumb and forefinger the two ends of the pieces of mono you want to join. Let's call the piece with its long end to the right line A, the other piece of line B. About 3 inches of each end of each line should protrude over the other.

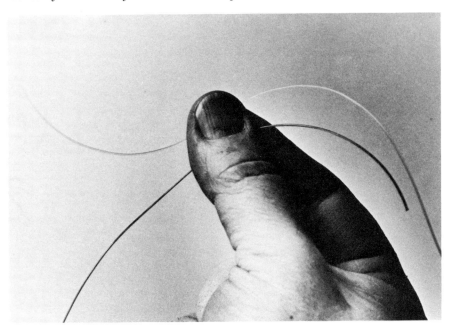

need a full 3 inches of loose end on each piece. With the left hand, wrap the loose ends of line A around the standing portion of line B, and the loose end of B around the standing portion of A. Keep holding the center loop open with your right thumb and forefinger.

Now, slip a match or twig into that loop, forcing it in by letting up a bit on the pressure of your right thumb and finger. Grasp the standing portion of line A—on your left side—with your left hand and gently work your right thumb and forefinger off the loop. Don't pull on either piece of the mono. The pressure of the wrapped ends will hold the match or twig in place while you slip the ends of the two lines into the loop beside it; line A from the top, line B from the bottom. Pull gently on both lines at the same time until they slide together. Now, you can slip out the match or twig without losing the knot.

Do this, and your forming knot will resemble the one in the photo. Just keep pulling the two lines together steadily and the knot will shape

Wrap the protruding end of line A over line B and vice versa, taking three turns with each end. The secret of making these wraps is to make them long, so the friction of one piece of mono against the other will hold the turns in place. Slip a match or small twig or weed stem into the gap you're still holding in your thumb and forefinger between line A and line B. Now you can let go with your right hand and the match will stay in place.

itself. Trim the tag ends off as close to the turns of the knot as you can manage. That's all there is to it.

If you get a mono line badly snarled and succeed in taking out the tangles but find the line still wants to twist, don't despair of ever straightening it out. Put a minimum weight, such as a snap or swivel, on the loose end. If you're on a stream, look for a straight run of clear water, and pay the line out slowly, letting the current carry it downstream, until you're past the twisty section. Reel in slowly, putting no more pressure on the line than the current supplies. If you're fishing from a boat, pay the line out behind the boat while cruising at the slowest possible speed, and reel in as described above. You'll find that the twists have been removed and the line will again lay smoothly on your reel. I like to do my mono lines this way a couple of times a season, just to keep them from getting to the point where a twist will form of its own volition.

Hold the mono in one hand, use the other to bend the loose end of line A back over the turns and stick its tip into the gap held open by the match, feed it in from the top. Do the same thing with the tip of line B, feeding it up along the match from the bottom. Holding one line in each hand, pull them very slowly together. As the knot begins to form the match will fall out; if it doesn't, pull it out, it has served its purpose.

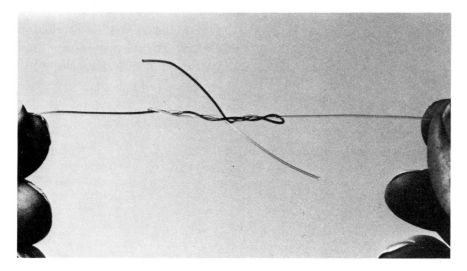

It's all downhill, now. Keep pulling the mono strands together gently and steadily and the knot will form itself. When it feels firm, wrap the mono around your hands and pull hard to clinch the knot. Trim the ends close to the knot. With very little practice, you can tie this knot blindfolded if you follow the method pictured.

When you encounter a problem with a fishing line, don't yield to your first angry impulse to throw the line away and buy a new one. Buy the new one, if it's in the middle of the season, but save the old line and use it to experiment with new knots, new ways of splicing, new kinds of material to mend frayed spots. There are a lot of discoveries waiting to be made. You just might be the one who makes them.

5

LURES

Although written histories of the angling arts give no clues to the exact date when fishermen first discovered that fish would attack an artificial lure, anthropologists have found that almost all primitive tribes, though living in widely separated geographical areas, practiced lure-fishing. Metal lures migrated across the Mediterranean from Egypt, where fishing was practiced as a sport rather than a means of garnering food as early as 3000 B.C. Such lures were used in Greece and Rome more than 1000 B.C., and presumably their use spread along the seacoasts in the direction of Spain, and then north to the shores of what is now France. Long before their recorded history began, the Scandinavian tribes used shell and bone lures both offshore and in the fjords; and in their far wanderings the Norsemen must have carried lures to other places.

Lure-fishing began to predominate U.S. angling about the middle of the 1800s, after George Snyder's multiplying reel had passed through several stages of development. About 1815, Dr. Thomas Buell, a Connecticut dentist, patented the first fishing lure to pass through the U.S. Patent Office, a wobbling spoon. But lures really began to come of age in the 1890s, when patent applications for the first plug-type wooden lures were filed by two tackle innovators, Jim Heddon and J. T. Lowe, on the same day. Heddon quickly put his "Dowagiac" plug into commercial production; Lowe did the same thing with his "Tango."

One reason for the instant popularity of "plug fishing" was that the new wooden plugs ended several problems that had plagued anglers using earlier metal lures that had to be retrieved fast or they would snag up. And the rotating metal lures could ruin a good silk line in a few hours of casting by kinking it up so badly that it could no longer be used. The new wooden plugs were buoyant and could be fished on the surface as well as at controlled depths; they could be retrieved slowly, and they did not twist lines.

Before inflation, few anglers considered it worthwhile to repair or restore lures. Of course, every fisherman has at one time or another gotten hooked on a pet lure just about as firmly as have the fish that this "hot" or "lucky" lure has brought to his net. When a fisherman becomes enamored with a lure he's come to consider unusually productive, he'll spend any amount of time and effort to keep that lure productive. He'll polish it, repaint it, adorn it with new hooks, and give it all kinds of tender loving care, even though he's probably got two or three others exactly like it in his tackle box.

More and more anglers are beginning to give all their lures this kind of attention. Lures do get damaged. They're dropped, stepped on, snagged on sunken limbs that bend or tear out hooks, their finish gets scratched on the sand of stream and lake beds and chipped by underwater encounters with sharp-edged rocks. The plating on metal lures rubs off and rust spots pop out like measles to ruin their glittering shine. Wire shafts on spinners get bent, clevises are pinched together, and the action of the lure is spoiled. But normal wear and tear combined with inattention—not careless handling or accidents—is the greatest enemy of lures. The answer isn't junking the lure, but restoring it to new condition.

Even with inflation, most lures are priced at less than $2. There's little reason to rework your lures if you're going to spend $25 or $30 on special tools and equipment; for that much money you can buy a couple of dozen new lures. The only sensible approach is to use commonplace, everyday tools.

The one tool essential to lure-tinkering that you might not already own is a pair of smooth-jawed roundnose pliers. These are often called rosary or looping pliers, and they're priced at about $4 to $5 a pair. This is a tool you ought to have in your kit anyhow, since these pliers are handy in many other tackle-tinkering applications. Chances are you already have all the other tools that should be in every lure fisherman's tackle box: split-ring pliers, wire-cutting pliers, a small ball peen hammer, a skill knife of some sort, a screwdriver or two.

Materials needed are felt pads, which you can get by chopping up an old hat, a household scouring pad, emery paper, crocus cloth, and fine sandpaper. When working on lures, one sheet of sandpaper goes a long way. Acrylic and epoxy enamels now come in spray cans, and are easily obtainable. Auto body shops usually mix more acrylic enamels than they use for touch-up jobs; make a deal with a local body shop, supply them with a number of small screw-top jars, and ask them to pour batches of leftover enamel in these jars and save it for you instead of dumping it.

Specialized tackle materials needed include clevises, lure wire, hooks, screw eyes, and hangers. Unless well-stocked tackle shops abound in the area where you live, you'll probably have to order these by mail. A list of suppliers is in the Appendix, and most of them will send you a catalog, either free or for 25 to 50 cents. But a couple of bucks will set you up for life with most of the small items you'll need— except for hooks. Good hooks are, as they always have been, the most expensive items tackle-tinkerers are called on to buy.

For the sake of convenience, I've arbitrarily divided lures into two major categories: thick-bodied and thin-bodied. The first group includes all plug-type lures made of wood or plastic; the second, all metal-bodied lures such as spinners, spoons, and wobblers or darters. A third group, the soft-bodied lures cast of plastic, has been omitted here because there's no way to repair or refurbish such lures; all you can do is replace them when they fade or melt or get chewed apart by a fish.

Size and weight aren't considered in my arbitrary classification, as these factors are incidental to type. A spinner-blade is a spinner-blade, whether it's as big as your hand or as small as your thumbnail; a plug is a plug, whether it's an inch long or a big hook-hung monster the size of a small baseball bat used for fish such as tarpon. Procedures that you'll use in repairing or refurbishing one size of lure in either family are the same—the only difference is the size of the items with which you'll be working.

Maintenance Common to All Lures

This can be reduced to a half-dozen words: keep lure bodies clean, hooks sharp. Both are jobs that ought to be done often, especially at streamside. A scrap of coarse cloth carried in your pocket or tackle box will take care of the cleaning. Linen cloth is ideal; it has a scoring action that you don't get from cloth woven of softer fibers. For sharpening hooks, a hook hone is worth ten times its weight in fish brought to net. You'll find the angle-sided hone very good for big hooks, the triangular tapered job is excellent for medium-size hooks, and the round one has a feature that is especially handy: a center hole through which a lanyard can be strung and attached to a shirt pocket button or a loop on a fishing jacket so that you can't lose the stone while you're fumbling around trying to sharpen a hook with wet, slippery fingers while wading.

Do learn to use a hook hone properly. The grooves these hones have will put the final touch on a hook point only if you pull the hook along the groove with the point in the direction of your pull. Use short forward strokes to sharpen the inner side, with the curve of the hook around the stone, then turn the hook over and pull it point-first through the groove, as shown.

Thick-bodied Lures

About the most common job you'll do in repairing a plug-type lure, short of a complete overhaul, is replacing its hooks. About half the lure manufacturers use hangers to attach the hooks to the lure, the other half use screw eyes. Replacing a hook installed with hangers is a job that calls for a screwdriver with a tiny blade, and isn't something you'd want to do while fishing. It's easier just to cut through the eye of the hook with your cutting pliers and put a new hook on with a split ring. This used to be about as tedious a chore as taking off and replacing a

A lot of anglers fail to hone their hooks on all sides, and wind up with burred points. Work the hook in the grooves of the hone, turning it to make sure you get a rounded point, and always pull the hook point-first along the groove.

hook hanger, but with split-ring pliers like those illustrated it can be done fast, without split fingernails or stabbed fingertips, even with wet hands. The picture shows how these pliers work.

Don't worry about the change to split rings changing the lure's action, the change might improve it. During many years of fishing, I've gotten acquainted with a few of the men who design, manufacture, and field-test lures, and I've learned that some of these fellows who originate lures can't believe any change will be anything but harmful. During those years, I've also encountered a number of fishermen using lures containing changes in hook type or placement that have improved

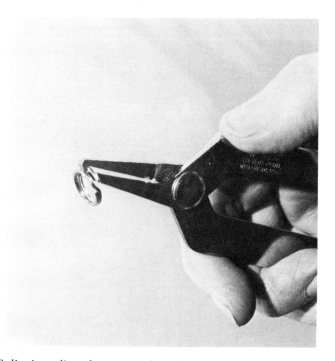

*Split-ring pliers have tips that slip into the space between
the turns of a split-ring and hold the sides apart while you
start a hook or snap.*

the lures substantially. Experimenting with different hook locations,
hook sizes, and methods of attaching them to a lure can often make a
great deal of difference in the way the lure brings fish to the net. The
experimenting you do might prove very helpful—not only to luremakers, but to fellow anglers.

Whether thick-bodied lures are made of wood or plastic, your
approach is the same. Your eyes will tell you when a lure needs
refinishing. It will begin to show cracks, like the lure pictured, or will
be marred with dents and scratches caused by accidents or just by
regular use. Your first job will be to strip the lure of its hardware. Use a
screwdriver if the hooks are attached with hangers or use the shank of
a hook like a lever, as shown, to take out screw eyes. From this point

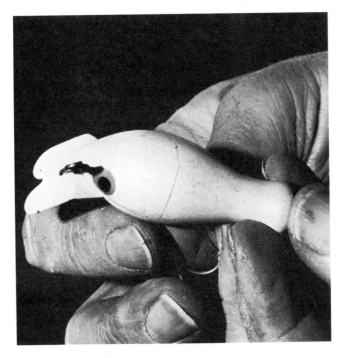

Big cracks like this in a plug's finish mean that in a very short time big chunks of the finish will begin popping off.

Use the hook shank as a lever to do a quick job of taking off hooks attached with screw eyes.

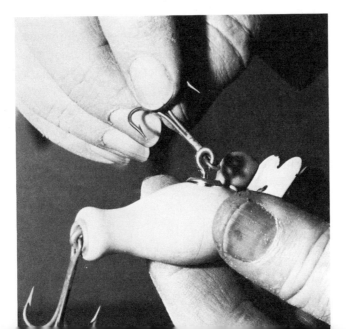

on, the skills you use will be those associated with any wood refinishing. Dunk the lure in paint remover and scrape it clean, fill any deep dents with epoxy, go over it with sandpaper, and then either by dipping or spraying apply an undercoat of the type called for by the kind of finish you plan to use, either acrylic or epoxy enamel. These are all straightforward operations that should cause no problems. Do be sure, though, to give the undercoat a final polishing with crocus cloth if you're going to use either acrylic or epoxy enamel, and to wipe it completely clean with a cloth moistened in thinners or turpentine before putting on the enamel.

In the manufacture of wooden plugs fitted with screw eyes, the eyes are often dipped in glue before being threaded into their pilot holes in the lure, and when you take them out the screw holes may be enlarged. Rather than using larger screw eyes, fill the old holes with epoxy, using a toothpick or wood splinter to get the glue all the way to the bottom of the hole. Then, before dipping the undercoated plug or spraying it with the finish coat of enamel, let the epoxy dry and redrill the pilot hole. For this you'll need a smaller drill bit than the $\frac{1}{16}$-inch size commonly sold in sets of shop bits. Most hardware stores stock wire-gauge bits, which graduate down to tiny bits no bigger in diameter than a hair. Take your screw eye with you to the store and get a wire-gauge bit of the proper size, one just a trifle smaller than the outside diameter of the screw threads.

While you can sometimes chuck such tiny bits into a power drill, this isn't always possible, and you might find it necessary to use a hand drill or a pin vise. Exacto makes an excellent pin vise, and there are others very similar that will take even hair-fine bits. You're really better off drilling the pilot holes by hand, because you'll have more complete control over the job; power drills often will break undersized bits no matter how delicately you use them. Though the bits aren't expensive, 30 to 40 cents each, there's no point in breaking one needlessly.

You may occasionally encounter plastic lures that have a metal plate or reinforcing strip of some sort running through their bodies, with the hook eyes and line eye permanently attached. You'll know when you run into lures made this way, because when you begin trying to unscrew the eyes you won't be able to budge them. Don't try to force them, you'll only break them. Just mask eyes and hooks with masking tape and go on with the refinishing. If a hook on a lure made like this has to be replaced, snip it off and put the new one on with a split ring.

Your only problem now is to get a dust-free finish when you apply the final coat of enamel. About the easiest way to assure yourself of a speckless final enamel coat is to duplicate in miniature the cabinets in which automobile body shops wheel cars for their final finishing. Get a big fiberboard carton and a length of stout wire or small dowel long enough to span it. Poke the wire through the carton horizontally and hang your lures on it, as shown, for spray painting or for drying if you dip-finish them. If you can't locate a suitable carton that still has its top attached, use masking tape to put a width of newspaper on the upper side in such a way that it can be folded down like a flap to cover the carton's open end.

Stick a length of stiff wire or small dowel through the sides of a cardboard carton to make a cabinet in which to spray paint lures or in which lures painted by dipping can drip and dry in a dustless atmosphere. If the carton has no top, make a cover by taping newspapers over it.

Whether you coat your lures by spraying or dipping, be sure to plug the freshly drilled screw-eye pilot holes with toothpicks or wood splinters before enameling. After the finish coat has dried, you can add any sort of decorations your imagination dictates: eyes, stripes, polka dots, strips of metallic tape, fluorescent tape, or whatever else you fancy. If you want lures that glitter, you can either sprinkle them with metallic flakes while they're still wet, or use one of the clear lacquer finishes that have flakes suspended in the liquid. Incidentally, for applying eyes, there are plastic squeeze bottles with nipplelike tops of different sizes that can be filled with paint and the tip touched to the lure to leave a perfect dot. And there's certainly nothing wrong with applying your decorative touches with a plain old-fashioned paintbrush.

As far as lure colors and decorations are concerned, I'll admit to being skeptical. For many years I used a set of eight plugs in plain solid-color finishes. Four of the plugs were lipped to run deep, four designed for surface or shallow-running fishing. One plug of each type was solid black, one was yellow, one light green, and one the traditional white body with a red head. I wasn't limiting myself from choice, because at that time light plugs were hard to find, and these were the only ⅜-ounce plugs I could dig up to use on a nice rod E. C. "Pop" Powell had made for me, which I wanted to use for fishing as well as tournament casting.

With my limited array of lures, I took just about as many bass as did my companions who carried several dozen. I've wondered ever since whether fancy-finished plugs aren't better fisherman-attractors than fish-attractors, and when I refinish plugs I usually wind up enameling them in a solid color without adding any special decorations.

If you're going to get into refinishing and refurbishing lures, take a tip from the manufacturers and set up a small production line. Wait until you've accumulated a half-dozen lures that need attention, and break down your operations into separate steps: preparation, cleaning, sanding, undercoating, polishing, refinishing. Carry all the lures through each step in one operation. If you want to paint them separately, use two cartons, one for spray painting, one for drying; if you finish by dipping, you'll need only one drying cabinet. Working this way, you can do a number of lures in only a little more time than it takes to refinish one.

Thin-bodied Lures

While thin-bodied lures cover a wider range of variations than do the plug-type, thick-bodied group, you don't need to be a skilled metalworker to handle repairs or to refurbish them. There are two basic kinds of lures in the thin-bodied group: one is the spoon, which has all its hardware attached to holes drilled in its body; the other is the shafted lure, which can be simply a spinner blade and hook on an eyed wire shaft, or a fairly complicated arrangement of a bead head, a spinner blade, and a metal body of bulletlike shape, with the hook back of the body.

Within these groupings there are an infinite number of variations, created by adding tufts of feathers or fur or threadlike rubber or plastic, by painting the bodies and decorating them, by fitting spinners both fore and aft, or by using a big spinner blade at the head and a fingernail-size fluttering spinner just above the hook. None of these extra touches changes the fact that the two basic types are spoons and spinners. Even trolling lures, which may be made up of a long string of spinner or spoon blades strung together on a single shaft or connected by separate shafts between each blade, require the same sort of repair procedures that are used on others of this big family.

You'll actually be performing only a limited number of special jobs: refinishing, replacing hardware, and forming new shafts. Refinishing may be simply a matter of polishing a spoon or spinner blade. Blades that are made of solid brass or copper generally need only to be cleaned with water and a household-type metal scouring pad; if the blade is very corroded, you may need to use some kind of metal polish. There are now polishes especially formulated to be effective on brass, copper, stainless steel, silver, and so on. Most of them contain an ingredient that acts chemically on the metal, to remove oxidation and stains. Just a quick rub over and rinse is all that's required to clean solid metal lures.

Plated metal lures are another matter. Tinplate, chrome plate, and nickel plate surfaces are usually applied on forms stamped from iron; brass was once widely used as a base for plated lures, but it's now too costly. When the plated surface of a sheet-iron lure gets badly corroded and begins to break down or peel off, leaving scabrous spots on the lure, there's very little choice left but to paint the blade or cover it

185

with one of the new metallic tapes that have pressure-sensitive acrylic adhesive backs.

If you're concerned about the durability of these tapes, or about the tape's ability to cling firmly to the metal blade, don't worry. These tapes have the same acrylic adhesive backing that's used to put identification numbers on jet planes and racing cars, and if the tape stays on a jet plane in a thunderstorm at 500 miles an hour, or on a racing car clipping along at 200 miles an hour, it'll stay on your spinner blade.

Resurfacing a blade with these tapes is easy. You don't even have to disassemble the spinner to do it. The tape is inexpensive; a piece that will cover more than fifty big spinner blades will cost about 1 cent per blade.

Your first job is to clean the spinner blade to which the tape is to be applied. Then cut a square or rectangle of tape large enough to cover the blade, and peel off the protective backing. Stick the tape on the spinner, put the spinner flat on a block of wood or piece of cardboard and trim off the excess tape with a craft knife or scissors. Press the tape down all around the spinner, working out from its center. There will be two or three places where because of the spinner's curve the tape will form into creases or wrinkles. If you work the tape properly when applying it, you can form these wrinkles and hole their number down to the two or three that will form no matter what you do.

Take the tip of your knife blade and slit down the center of each fold. Don't try to snip out a triangular piece, because you'll probably fail to match up the edges; this type of trimming is much trickier than you might think. But if you make just one straight cut down the center, you can overlap the edges of the cut, press the overlap flat, and these overlaps won't be noticed in the finished job. And that's it—the tape will stick until you scrape it off, in and out of the water. If you want to gussy up the job a bit, coat the taped spinner with a clear acrylic or polyurethane lacquer. Dipping is the easiest way to do this.

You can get these acrylic-backed tapes in a wide range of colors, including gold and silver, and can create two-toned spinners or three-toned or striped designs in an unlimited variety with a minimum outlay of time and money. At about 1 cent per spinner, it's a lot less expensive to cover worn spinner blades with tape than it is to buy new lures.

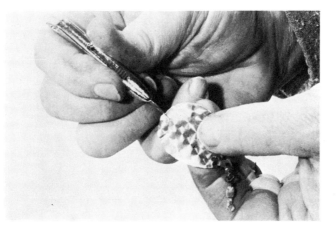

To remove the wrinkles that form in tape, hold the spinner blade as shown, then cut from the point at which the wrinkle begins in a straight line to the edge of the spinner. Use the tip of your knife to overlap the edges, then press them down firmly. The cut won't be invisible to your close inspection, but the fish won't notice it.

Rebuilding a lure isn't a terrible job. You can buy preformed shafts—that is, short lengths of lure wire with one eye formed—but you're going to have to learn to form one eye, and it's just as easy to form two once you've gotten the knack. Besides, you can buy a 25-foot roll of lure wire, which will provide shafts for about seventy-five lures, for about as much as you'd pay for twenty-four preformed shafts. Lure wire is made of either stainless steel or nickel steel, and is more flexible and easier to work than piano wire. It is measured in diameters of hundredths of an inch, and the most useful diameters are .024 and .026.

If you're just beginning to work with lure wire, the easiest way to start forming loops is with a jig. This doesn't have to be anything fancy, just a 20- or 30-penny nail, driven into a piece of scrap lumber and the head sawed off with a hacksaw and the stump filed smooth. This kind of jig raises your work about 2½ inches from the surface of

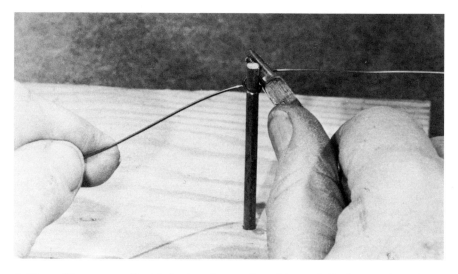

A 20- or 30-penny nail with its head cut off and its end filed smooth makes a fine jig on which to bend eye-loops in wire leaders and lure body shafts. To start an eye, wrap an end of a piece of lure wire around the nail.

the board, as shown, which gives you more working space than do most commercial bending jigs. It also costs a lot less.

When you first begin learning the simple knack of bending lure wire, leave yourself a lot of spare length at the end being bent. It's easier to work with. Later, you can cut down on this waste and work with smaller lengths.

Start your eye-loop by making one overlapping turn of lure wire around the nail, as illustrated. Hold the working end of the wire with a pair of pliers—flat-jawed duckbills are being used in the picture, but any pliers will do this job—and using the wire shaft as a fulcrum, wrap the end around the shaft as close to the point of overlap as possible. You can work a lot closer with flat-jawed pliers than you can with more conventional types. If you use pliers with big jaw ends, you'll be working by feel, while flat-jawed pliers let you watch what you're doing.

In wrapping the end of the wire around the shaft, keep a firm, even tension on it. Move the entire pliers in one circular motion rather than

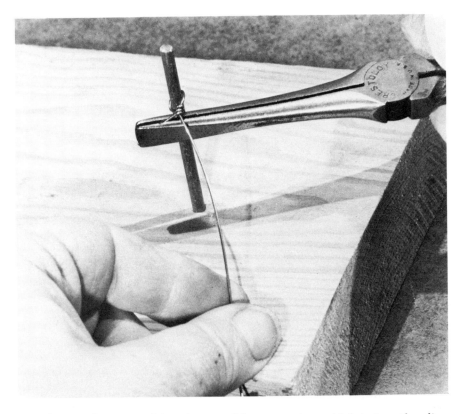

Use the standing part of the wire as a fulcrum against which to turn the pliers holding the end. Three tight turns close the loop.

making the turn a little bit at a time. This means grasping the end of the wire below the shaft and turning the hand in which you hold them without releasing the end of the wire. Three turns is enough to make a secure eye in any weight wire. Trim off the end with cutters as close to the shaft as possible.

Forming an eye-loop using two pairs of pliers is just about as easy as it is to form them on a jig. To form eye-loops with pliers, you need a pair of round-jawed pliers, with a tapering nose. The pair illustrated are a type I've never seen duplicated; they were given me by a luremaking friend many years ago, and though I've tried to find another pair like

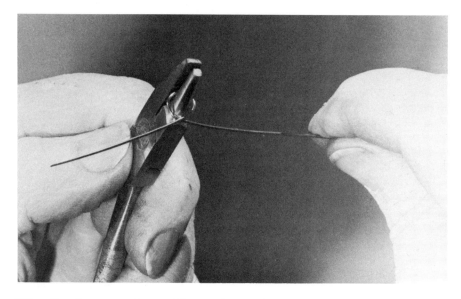

When forming an eye-loop with roundnose pliers, make the same starting turn you would if using a jig; bring the end of the wire around to almost a 180-degree angle.

them, I've never been able to. But a regular pliers with round jaws is the kind used by most luremakers.

Grasp the wire in the pliers and make a turn around one jaw, as shown in the photo. Then, holding the work firmly in the roundnose pliers, make three twists around the shaft using other pliers to pull the end of the wire down on the left-hand side, up on the right-hand side, and again over to the left in one motion. Trim the wire with cutters. The end result, whether you've formed it on a nail-jig or on a pair of roundnose pliers, will be a perfect eye-loop.

If you must rebuild a lure for any reason, start with an eye-loop, then put on a bead, either a regular round or oval bead or one of the small metal beads called "unies." The bead between eye and clevis serves as a washer; the clevis, a C-shaped bit of metal with holes at each end of it through which the shaft passes, is likely to jam against the loop forming the eye unless this bead washer is included. Next, put the new clevis on the spinner. Be sure you put the spinner on the clevis

190

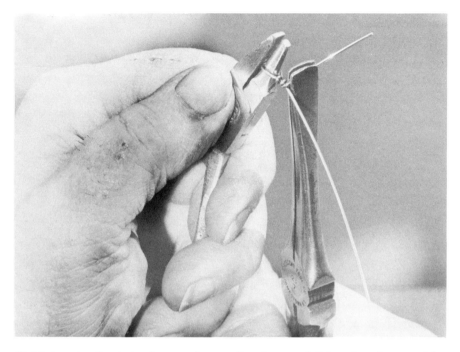

Hold the wire firmly in the roundnose pliers in your left hand and wrap with a second pair held in your right. It's a knack quickly acquired by practicing.

so that its convex side will face the eye-loop. The clevis on the spinner will have its top end toward the eye-loop.

Thread beads or the lure body on the shaft, then make the first turn in forming a loop and slip a hook into the circle; it will rest beside the nose of the pliers while the turns that complete the loop are being made. If you want a lure on which you can change hooks easily, just form the bottom loop and hang the hook on with a split ring.

As you can see, there's really only one tricky job you'll need to learn in rebuilding—or, for that matter, building—wire-shafted lures, and that job is forming an eye-loop. If you use a nail-jig such as was pictured earlier, you'll have to drive in different sizes of nails to form loops of different diameters; if you work with taper-nosed round-jawed pliers you can adjust the loop size by working at the tip of the jaws in forming small loops, at the base to form big ones.

191

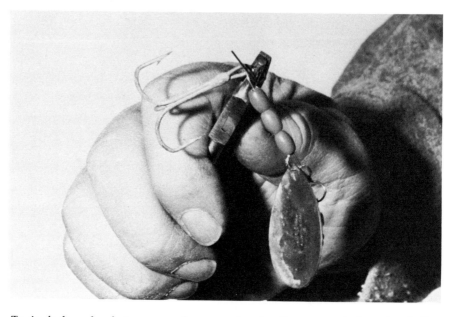

To include a hook in an eye-loop, make the first turn of the wire before threading it on. Then form the eye.

Refurbishing spoon-family lures is even easier than working with lures built on wire shafts. The hooks, swivels, and other hardware fitted on spoon-family lures all go on with split rings. Manufacturers often fasten hooks and swivels to lures of this family with solid rings, and when you want to rebuild one you'll have to cut the rings; usually, a small cold chisel is needed, because most cutting pliers don't provide enough leverage to cut the rings.

But all the other procedures are the same: cleaning, painting, or refinishing with tape, and so on.

With a few simple tools, a minimum investment in materials, a little bit of time, and the wire-working skill you'll acquire with practice, you can repair almost any damage to any lure. Restoring lures and keeping them at their best is just as important as refurbishing all the other components of your angling gear. After all, it's the lure that attracts the fish.

6

ACCESSORIES

Every year it gets a little bit tougher to draw the line between items of tackle that are really essential to fishing and those that make things just a little easier or more convenient—in one word, luxuries. The essentials in the accessories category make up a rather long list: landing nets and gaffs, waders, wading sandals, and wading staffs, creels and tackle boxes, rod cases and fisherman's cutlery. All these items are used universally by fishermen, whether they fish from the shore, a boat, or wade out into a stream.

Perhaps the hardest lesson a fisherman must learn is to be prepared for anything. This doesn't necessarily apply to the fellow who confines himself to close-by, familiar waters that he fishes regularly. He's pretty well aware of the conditions he'll encounter, and can cut his gear requirements to a minimum. I've done a fair amount of this kind of fishing and it's very relaxing to set out for a fishing spot only four or five miles away, carrying nothing but a rigged-up rod, a net, and creel, certain that in your pockets you've got everything else you're going to need.

More mobile fishermen can't do this, especially if they're going into strange territory or setting out from an end-of-the-road camp for even more isolated waters. At these times, getting to a tackle shop may involve an all-day trip, and even returning to camp means hiking several miles. The fisherman operating in a situation such as this must be prepared to handle minor repairs to his gear at streamside, or at best in camp, and obviously any major repair job is going to have to wait until the trip's over.

You can certainly find room in a pocket for a small poptop plastic capsule. In it, carry a modest assortment of reel screws—not forgetting a bail-retaining screw if you're using a spinning reel—and a few of the tiny screws that hold together the frames and bows of your optical glasses or sunglasses. I would also include in any tackle box or fishing shirt or jacket that goes to an isolated stream a spare spooled line for fly rod or spinning rod, an extra pawl for the baitcasting reel, some rubber bands, a couple of needles and a pair of tweezers. These are all items that I've needed more than once on long days away from base camp, and I don't think it includes anything that I haven't used since I started carrying an emergency kit.

Landing Nets

In the section of the country where I'm living now, old-timers have a phrase that describes the kind of deterioration to which landing nets are subject. When an object that on the surface looks sound suddenly gives way, they say "it's rottened out." Landing net bags have a habit of rottening out while they still look stout and viable. You don't become aware that the cords of the bag have deteriorated until that moment when a fish plunges on through the net while you're lifting it out of the water.

This happens as often to net bags made from plastic cordage as it does to those made of linen or cotton mesh. Sunlight is the enemy of most plastics; it's the sun's ultraviolet rays that cause mono lines and leaders to weaken and break, and the same rays do their work on net bags. Regardless of the material—be it cloth or plastic—from which the bag of your landing net is made, at the first sign of a break in one of them, replace the bag.

It's not much of a job to replace a net bag, just how much depends on whether the frame is bolted or swaged into the handle. Most newer

Fit a new bag to the frame of a landing net by using short pieces of masking tape to hold the loops on the frame while you're positioning the bag. Then begin fastening the loops at the throat of the frame. Tie a small slip-knot with a square knot tied to the standing portion of the lacing cord to form the noose. This is your anchor knot, and goes as closely to the throat as you can manage.

195

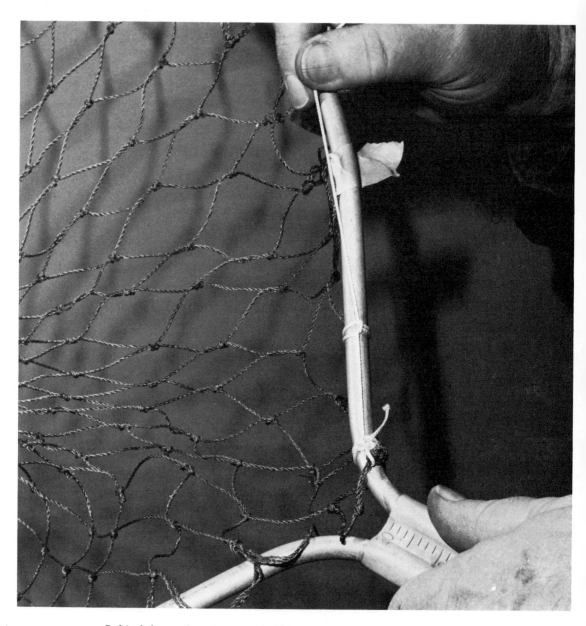

Behind the anchor tie, use a half-hitch to hold the first loop of the bag in place, then lace on the other loops with the simple loop knots pictured. When you've worked around the frame, tie off in the same way you tied the beginning loop.

nets have bolts or sheet metal screws holding handle and frame together, most older aluminum-framed nets have handles into which the frame ends are swaged. Where bolts or screws secure the joint, it's a simple matter to take one of the frame ends out, slide off the old bag, and slide on the new. Swaged joints can't be opened, so when replacing the bag on a net having this type of frame-to-handle construction the new bag's going to have to be lashed on.

Fitting the bag properly is the most tedious part of the job. Use short strips of masking tape to fit the new bag to the frame so that it will be uniform in spacing of its loops, as illustrated. When you've got the spacing arranged to your satisfaction, anchor the back loop with a square-knot slip noose, and use a simple thread-through loop knot to secure each bag loop that is attached to the frame. Tie off with another square-knot slip noose anchored by a second square knot tied over the noose itself.

Wooden-frame landing nets have become collector's items, but if you own or acquire one, and need to replace the net bag, it's a tedious but simple job. These nets have holes on opposite sides of the throat and other holes through the center of the frame spaced regularly around the frame's perimeter. The bags of these nets are invariably bunched at the throat. To replace a bag, equip yourself with a length of heavy braided line—about 50-pound squidding or ocean trolling line, long enough to go around the outside of the frame—and a piece of fairly small-diameter wire 3 to 4 inches long. Copper wire is both firm and flexible, and is ideal.

Start the job by tying one end of the heavy braided line with a simple square knot around any top loop of the bag. Push the free end of the heavy line through either of the holes on one side of the frame throat. Form the wire into a loop, and use it as you would a needle. Pick up each top loop of the bag in turn and pull the loop through one of the holes in the frame far enough to thread the heavy line through the loop of the bag. When you've worked your way around the frame, you'll probably have anywhere from three to six top loops of the bag left with no holes in the frame to go through. Thread the braided line through the hole in the throat, pass it through the surplus loops, and tie it off on the beginning end of itself with a square knot. Go fishing.

Gaffs and Tailers

Once upon a time a gaff was an oversized barbless hook set with a pinned ferrule at the end of a wooden handle. Like so many angling accessories, gaffs have changed. Today, they're usually made from a length of hollow aluminum tubing filled with flotation material, the tubing sealed at one end by a tapped metal plug into which the hook is screwed and at the other end by a molded rubber or plastic handgrip to which a lanyard is attached. The wood-handled gaff has gone the way of the silkworm gut leader.

The newest addition to the gaff family is a spring-loaded job made by Auto-Gaff in Rhode Island. This gaff is set for operation by pulling on its hook, which has a 4-inch travel. The hook is released by a trigger just below its handle, and has a reference mark on the hook shaft to guide you in putting it below the fish. These gaffs must be returned for factory service if they should ever need repairs, Auto-Gaff advises.

Maintaining any gaff is a matter of keeping its business end sharp. If you encounter a wood-handled gaff (and I tried vainly to find one for pictures) on which you want to replace a splintery handle, the hook will probably be set into the handle with a pinned metal ferrule, just like a garden rake or hoe is set. Remove the pin, rasp and sand the new

Typical gaffs, like the one at the bottom of the picture, are of tubular aluminum filled with a flotation material, slip-on handle, and a solid plug at the business end threaded to accept the hook. The Auto-Gaff, at the top, requires factory service when repairs are needed or a new hook must be installed.

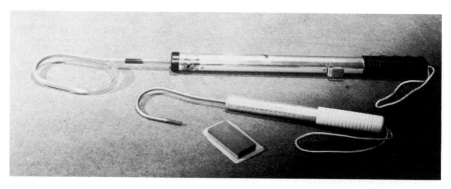

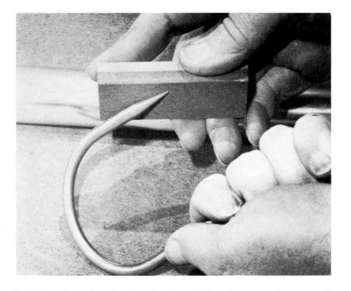

Gaffs having circular hooks should be sharpened by passing the whetstone down from the point in long smooth strokes, and working around the entire circumference of the hook. This results in a needle-sharp point free from burrs.

To sharpen the patented triangular-pointed hook of the Auto-Gaff, work the whetstone along each flat side in turn, working the stone away from the tip of the hook.

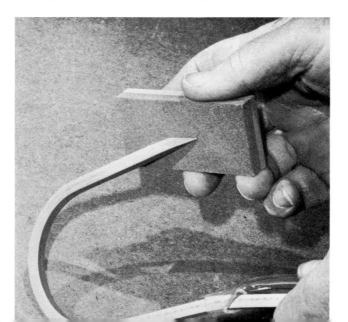

handle down to fit the ferrule, drive the blunt end of the hook into the handle, and repin the ferrule.

Hooks on metal-handled gaffs screw into a metal plug swaged into the bottom of the handle, and putting in a new hook is a matter of unscrewing the old hook and screwing in a new one.

There's a trick to sharpening a gaff hook, though. Use a small whetstone on a circular hook, and work from the point toward the bend with long, even strokes. If you work around the hook, it'll never get sharp; if you work toward the hook, you'll wind up with a burred instead of a needle-sharp point. The hook on the Auto-Gaff is triangular shaped, its makers point out, "like a shark's tooth." This hook should be honed with the whetstone flat to each of its sides in turn, again moving the stone away from the point, toward the hook's bend.

Tailers, like gaffs, have changed, too. Hand-operated tailers are being replaced by automatic ones. A hand-operated tailer is nothing but a length of fine strong wire fixed at one end of a shaft and running through loops or screw eyes or in a channel inside the shaft itself. In use, the wire is extended to form a noose that is dropped over the tail of the fish; lifting the tailer tightens the noose. The only repair job these tailers need is replacement of its wire. Spring-loaded, trigger-operated trailers that function much as does the automatic gaff just described must be sent in for factory service.

Waders and Boots

If you do your fishing in streams that don't require felt-soled boots or waders, all you're concerned about is keeping your wading gear stored properly between fishing trips and mending any rips or holes it might suffer. If you fish in waters where moss and algae collect on rocks and logs and make felt soles necessary, you're going to be faced sooner or later with resoling. It's not an involved or tricky job, so you needn't worry about it. Let's look first at between-use storage of your rubber or plastic wading togs.

Sunlight is the enemy of both rubber and plastic, heat in addition is an enemy of rubber, and both materials benefit by being stored in a way that will allow them to rest without being creased or compressed.

S-shaped hangers are the most satisfactory method of storing boots and boot-foot waders; stocking-foot waders shouldn't be draped over a coat hanger, but suspended by their suspender buckles; for this, you can clip the bottom bar out of a wire coathanger and bend a U into the ends over which the buckles can be slipped.

When you rip a pair of rubber boots or waders, the remedy is a patch just like those used on inner tubes. If you're lazy, the friendly service station where you buy your gasoline can do the job, but it's a three-minute matter at best to do it yourself. The old routine of scraping and scrubbing is done now by solvents. After locating the break, swab a small area around it first with buffing solvent, then with solvent and cleaner. Both solutions come in large and small cans, and the second solution should be swabbed only over the area that will be covered by the patch.

Patches come in assorted sizes and shapes, and before applying the second solvent solution, select a patch that will cover the break. The second solvent activates the bonding coating that is on the inner side of the patch, protected by a cloth backing, which must be peeled off. The outside of the patch is covered with a thin plastic film to make the final step in application easier. After peeling the backing off the patch, press it into place over the break and roll it or tap it with a hammer while the patched area rests on a firm, level surface. Finally, tear off the transparent plastic film over the patch.

If the break in your rubber wading gear is in a spot that's subjected to bending, or a place crossed at any point by a seam in the boot or wader material, you'll be wise to look on a cold-patch repair such as the one just described as a temporary expedient. It might hold forever without giving you any trouble, but it might not. Take your boots or waders to a tire service center and ask them to take off the cold patch and replace it with a hot vulcanized patch. This type of patch was commonplace in the days when all tires had inner tubes; it was available in kits, just as cold-patch equipment is today. But the old-fashioned hot patch is making a comeback, though at present it's available only at tire service centers.

Repairing plastic waders is even simpler than putting on a rubber cold patch. You use the same materials that are sold in kits in most variety stores for patching plastic wading pools and air mattresses. A

To set the patch firmly, roll it or tap it with a wood block or hammer, paying special attention to the edges.

kit costs about $1, and will contain four to six sheets of patching material and, if the material requires a catalyst, a supply of this solution. Most of the polyvinyl chloride plastic repair kits use plain tap water as a catalyst, so if you can find one of these, it'll save you a bit of trouble.

Applying the plastic patch differs only slightly from the application of a rubber cold patch. First, locate and mark the break or torn place. Cut a rounded-cornered piece of patching material of the size and shape required to cover the break and the area for about 1 inch all around it. Peel off the backing paper. You'll be left holding a piece of almost transparent plastic film, which is the patch. The instructions that come with the kit will tell you whether the kit contains a catalyst, or whether water is the catalyst. Whichever is indicated, dip the film in it, being sure to change the position of your fingers holding the patch while it's immersed so that all of the film will come into contact with the catalyst. Put the patch over the area you've marked, and use the smooth back of the backing paper to massage the wet film into complete contact with the area being patched. Let the patch dry; this will take about ten minutes.

Now, turn the waders or boots inside out far enough to expose the inner surface of the patched area and repeat the procedure you've just followed to apply an inside patch just a bit larger than the one you put on the outside. This is insurance. That plastic patching film is very thin, and waders and boots get a shearing or pulling type of stress that puts more strain on them than a wading pool or air mattress gets. Put on a double patch just to be sure you'll be fishing with dry feet the next time you use the waders.

Replacing felt soles on waders, wading sandals, or boots is a job some overcautious anglers hesitate to undertake. They can't bring themselves to believe that there's nothing arcane about a process that bonds two such dissimilar materials as rubber and felt so that they'll stay together while being walked on underwater. There isn't really anything mysterious about it, it's all in the adhesive used. You can get the materials you need in kit form from Fritz von Schlegell's outdoor outfitting supply house in Los Angeles, from George Uyeno's shop in Denver, and from Hille's in Williamsport, Pennsylvania. There are probably others who handle the kits, but these are the three I know about.

There's really no reason for you to back away from the resoling job. The hardest part of it comes first, cutting away the old felts, because they can't just be yanked off with a gentle tug. Use a linoleum knife if you have one, it'll make the cutting easier. When the old soles have been removed, clean the soles of the boots with a file or rasp to get off all old adhesive and to give the new adhesive a good surface to bond to.

Next, put each boot on the felt and trace its outline with chalk or a white marking pencil. Then spread a smooth layer of adhesive over the surfaces of the boot bottoms, carrying the adhesive out to their edges. Lay the boots on their sides, out of the way, where the adhesive-coated soles won't come into contact with each other or with anything else. The adhesive used in this job sticks instantly and rather permanently to any other surface that is covered with it. Put a coating of adhesive on the surface of the felt that will be bonded to the boots. Let the soles and boots rest for an hour or so after they've been coated; a

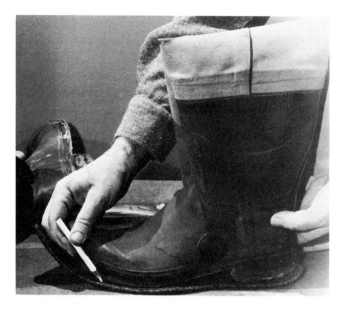

Trace the outline of each boot foot on the felt; use a white marking pencil or chalk if you're working with dark felt.

couple of hours won't do any harm, if you have something else to do.

Before you start the actual bonding of boots and felts, tear open a big brown paper bag, or get a piece of thick brown wrapping paper. Put a hammer or a stout block of wood where it will be handy.

Place a boot on the paper, sole down. It won't stick to the paper, so don't worry. Fold back an edge of the paper while you align the boot with the outline you've traced on the felt. When you're sure you're on the mark, outline and boot sole squarely together, tilt the boot forward at the toe without moving it in relation to the felt and roll the paper forward from the heel toward the toe. Press the back of the heel down firmly to bring it into contact with the felt. Roll the paper forward a bit more, until you can reach under the felt and pull it back with your fingers to bring it into contact with the vertical inner face of the heel, just back of the arch. Press felt and boot into firm contact, then take out the paper shield and push the rest of the boot sole into contact with

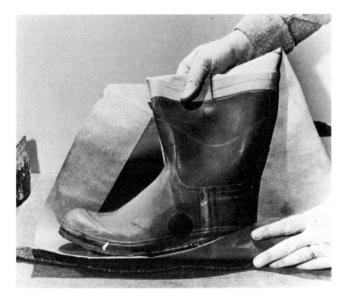

Put a sheet of thick paper between the felts and boots when fitting them. The surfaces coated with adhesive bond on contact if they touch. Fold back an edge of the paper to see how to place the boots within the marked outlines.

the felt. Do this with a smooth forward movement so the felt won't wrinkle.

Turn the boot sole-up and pound the sole with the hammer or block of wood. Don't spare the beating; the better job you do of making a firm contact between felt and boot, the better and more permanent their attachment will be. Repeat the bonding procedure with the second boot.

Put the boots on a working surface, an old plank or something of that kind, and trim off the excess felt around the edges of their soles and heels, as illustrated. Finally, put on the boots and tramp around in them for ten to fifteen minutes on a concrete surface, occasionally stamping your feet the way you'd like to do when you get angry if you weren't afraid people would think you're being childish.

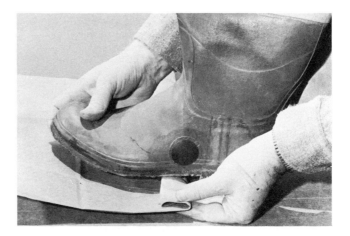

Press down on the toe of the boot when ready to attach the felts, and with your free hand roll the paper from between the felt and boot heel. Push the heel down onto the felt, it will stick at once. Lift the boot, letting the paper fall free and the front part of the felt dangle while you pull it up into the instep and smooth it along the front of the sole.

Pound the felt with a hammer or block of wood; cover every square inch of the surface to get good contact.

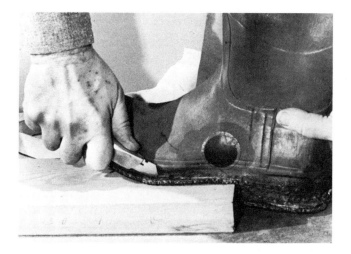

Rest the boot on a block of wood while you trim off excess felt.

Usually, the thick felt material used on waders will stand up for two or three years of hard service. When I was wearing felt-soled waders for three to four hours a day almost every day on the rough-bottomed steelhead rivers of the Pacific Northwest, I figured on getting two seasons of wear from a set of felts. Felt-soled waders have replaced old-style hobnail-studded wading footwear because the felts not only give you better footing, they give you better service. And when you're wading on mossy rocks or any kind of slick bottom, the assurance felt soles give you, the extra margin of safety they provide, make them worth the little bit of trouble they are to install.

Wading Staffs

A lot of fishermen refuse to carry wading staffs because they're afraid they'll be branded as cowards. Now, a wading staff is no firm guarantee that you won't get a ducking, any more than a painstaking physical examination on Monday guarantees you against suffering a cerebral hemorrhage on Tuesday. A wading staff does help you avoid a lot of duckings you might take without it, though. It took only one look at a machismo-minded angler who'd laughed at wading staffs as a crutch for cowards to make a believer of me; I saw him as he was taken from a big, brawling river after having been on the bottom for five days. On strange streams, and on big and dangerous but familiar ones, I've been saved dozens of times by that firm third leg my wading staff provides.

Most of the practical wading staffs I've seen have been made of metal, usually standard-wall aluminum conduit ¾ inch in diameter. Those made of thin-wall conduit are a bit lighter in weight, but tend to be a bit soupy in use. The standard staff—if there is such a thing—is 50 inches long, has a cork or plastic grip with a ring to which a long lanyard can be attached, and is weighted at the bottom end. The tip is usually blunted metal, not rubber or sharply pointed. Under extreme stress, these staffs will bend, and once the material of which they're

When the first coat of epoxy has dried, apply a second coat to the same surfaces. Slip the ends of the tubing into the connector and crimp with an adjustable-jaw wrench such as the ViseGrip being used in the photo. Set the jaws to close just enough to crimp the connector into good contact with the tubing, and turn the work to crimp in several spots. The staff will be ready for use as soon as the glue dries.

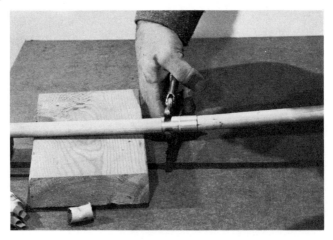

made has been bent there's no point in trying to bend it straight, because all you'll do is damage it further.

Mending such a staff is a fast and simple job. Just saw out the bent section with a hacksaw, file the ends square, apply a thin coating of epoxy to the sawed ends, carrying it about 1 inch up the staff, and let the glue dry. At the same time, put a thin coating of epoxy on the inner walls of a standard conduit connector and put it aside to dry. Aluminum is a metal that oxidizes very rapidly, and when it's being joined with epoxy the most satisfactory way to get a good bond is to precoat the surfaces to be joined. After the precoating is dry, put on a second coat, slip the ends of the tubing into the connector and crimp the connector gently with a preset locking wrench. As soon as the second glue coat has set, the staff can be used.

Rod Cases

Many otherwise conservative and eminently sensible anglers look on rod cases as a nuisance, as merely excess baggage. You'll see them carrying their rods unprotected, often not even unjointed, bending them into a car's trunk or passenger compartment. As a result, these fishermen break up a lot more rods than do those who take the few minutes required to unjoint a rod and slide it into a case. Any decent rod deserves this much respect, and if the rod is an exceptionally fine one, the protection a case gives it is even more important.

A good rod case, one made of thick-wall aluminum or high-impact reinforced plastic, will survive almost any kind of rough treatment it will get during normal use, and so will the rod inside it. The only care you'll have to give a good case is to keep the threads of its top clean if it has a screw-on cover, or replace the rubber caps if it's closed this way. With age, these caps lose elasticity and tend to slip off accidentally.

Thin-wall aluminum cases usually have two weaknesses. One is their caps. Most cases of this type have stamped caps of the same thin material from which the case is made, and these get cross-threaded very easily, and when cross-threaded they crack out and will no longer hold. All you can do with a case having a battered cap, such as the one illustrated, is to discard the cap and replace it with the slip-on rubber type.

Repeated cross-threading, a problem common to die-formed threads, results in the caps of thin-wall aluminum rod cases getting cracked and broken like this one.

Remove dents from aluminum rod cases by using a length of water pipe as an anvil. Chuck the pipe in a vise as in the photo and tap the dent out, holding the case in firm contact with the pipe.

Thin-wall cases are fairly easily dented, too, but this can be cured. Get a piece of 1½- or 1¾-inch standard water pipe long enough to reach into the area where the case is dented. Chuck the pipe in a vise, or fix it firmly to a workbench with wood blocks held by carpenter's clamps, and slide the rod case over it. With a light hammer and using very gentle tapping blows, begin working the dent out while holding the case down firmly on the pipe, which has become an improvised anvil. Tap from the edges of the dent toward the center, turning the case to keep its inner wall in contact with the pipe. A fiber hammer is even better than a machinist's hammer, since it won't mar the metal of the case, but unless you get too ambitious with your tapping, a few minutes work will see the dent removed. Buff the case later to hide any marks the hammer might leave.

To mend a very bad dent that covers a large area of the case, or to mend a break in the wall, splicing is necessary. Unfortunately, there aren't any 2-inch sleeves manufactured to fit over a rod case, but the repair is very much like the one just covered to a wading staff. In this instance, though, you'll have to make your own sleeve.

First, you'll have to remove the damaged section to see what length the sleeve will have to be. Do this with a fine-tooth blade in a hacksaw, using very light pressure and smooth, even strokes, since this metal bends very easily. Assuming that you want to wind up with your case the same length, measure the piece removed. You can shorten or lengthen the case if you wish, by changing the width of the sleeve.

Cut your sleeve from sheet aluminum approximately the same gauge (thickness) as the case. You'll actually need two sleeves. The inner sleeve will be equal in length to the circumference of the case and equal in width to the length of the piece removed from the case. This is the inner sleeve; the outer sleeve will be 1 inch wider than the inner sleeve and 2 to 2½ inches longer.

Before fitting the sleeves, true up the ends of the case if necessary. Use a square to check and make sure that they're not slanting off at an angle and if necessary true them with a fine-tooth file. Check both sleeves to be sure their edges are parallel and their corners form true 90-degree angles. Use a file to correct these, if it's necessary to do so.

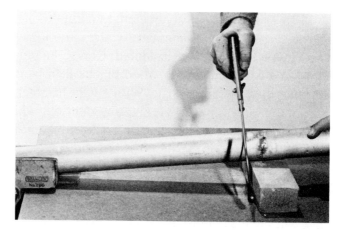

Saw out the damaged section of the rod case. It will be replaced by a splice that will keep the case the same length, or you can make it longer or shorter.

Prepare two rectangular aluminum plates according to directions given in the text, tacking the smaller plate to the larger as the photo shows. Then, bend the joined plates into a half-round shape.

Apply a thin even coat of epoxy on one side of each sleeve and on the area 1½ inches from the sawed edge of each piece of the rod case. Let this dry completely. (Remember, in joining aluminum to aluminum with epoxy, you need this base coat to assure a good bond; in effect, you'll be gluing epoxy to epoxy when you make the final joining.)

On the coated surface of the small sleeve, apply a coat of epoxy about ⅛ inch wide along one short edge. Butt this edge to the center of the large sleeve as shown in the picture, let the glue dry, then bend the joined sleeves into a half-circle or three-quarter as illustrated in the same photo. Then, put a generous coating of epoxy on the outer edges of the large sleeve, working a little of the glue under the small sleeve.

Slip a large hose clamp over each end of the rod case as shown; be sure you use the screw-up type illustrated. Butt the ends of the rod case against the inner sleeve as shown in the picture, and bend the outer sleeve so that it encircles the case. When you do this, the inner sleeve will of necessity be forced into the same diameter as the rod case; it will slip along the inside of the larger sleeve as it is bent into position.

Slide the hose clamps over the outer sleeve and tighten them. Use the screwdriver alternately on first one clamp, then the other. You may need to adjust the ends of the sleeve as the pressure from the clamps increases. You will have to twist the outer sleeve to keep it straight, and when you feel the outer sleeve closing tightly against the rod case, quickly check the two pieces of the case to be sure they are butting against the inner sleeve. Stop drawing the hose clamps tight when they are in full contact with the rod case around its entire circumference. If you have tightened the clamps alternately with only a few turns of the screwdriver on each clamp at a time, your inner sleeve will have the ends of the rod case butted to it, both the inner sleeve and the outer sleeve will be glued to the outer wall of the rod case, and the inner sleeve will also be glued to the outer sleeve. The final step is to wipe away the epoxy that's oozed out of the joint and set the work aside until the glue dries. If you're making a very long splice, use three or more clamps—enough to keep bulges from forming as the outer sleeve is drawn up.

This sleeving operation goes a lot faster in the doing than it appears to in the writing. It will result in a strong rod case, as strong and sturdy as the case was when new.

Slip a screw-type hose clamp over each section of the rod case. Butt the ends of the case as illustrated against the small inner plate, with the ends of the case resting on the epoxy-coated margins of the larger plate.

Bend the two plates simultaneously to encircle the rod case loosely. Hold the plates in place with one hand, use the other to slide the hose clamps over them from each end. Don't tighten the clamps excessively; when glue oozes from under the outer sleeve and the sleeve has come into full contact with the pieces of the rod case, quit tightening.

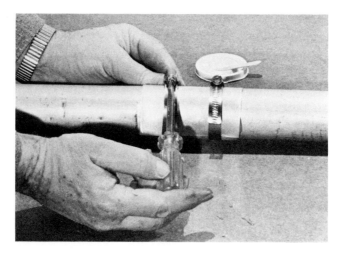

Just how successful this method of sleeving would be if used on a plastic rod case, I can't say; I've never tried it. While epoxy is supposed to glue anything to anything, there are some plastics which seem immune to any kind of glue, even the cyanoacrylate monomer glues discussed earlier. However, a sleeving repair using pop rivets to hold the sleeve in place would almost certainly be practical to use on a plastic case.

There are also fiberglass rod cases, and these can be repaired by using strips of fiberglass tape applied with the resin used in fiberglass fabrication. Boat dealers usually have kits that contain the materials needed to fix a fiberglass boat, and these can be used to repair anything else made of fiberglass except tubular rods—applying thick strips of fiberglass tape to a rod would ruin its action. The process is simple. A strip of fiberglass tape is dipped in a catalyst-activated resin, the surface to be repaired is brushed with the resin and the tape applied, smoothed into place, and another coat of the resin brushed on. Any repair kit you buy will contain detailed instructions.

Creels, Live-bags, and Tackle Boxes

Traditional woven willow or rattan creels are having a revival as more and more anglers discover that there's really no substitute for them. When wading a stream or lake or moving along the bank of either, a creel serves better than anything else to keep the mobile angler's fish in good condition. The rubberized plastic shoulder knapsacks sold in many tackle stores as creels will ruin fish by packing them into a hot, wet, airless mass where they will begin to spoil quickly. Fishermen operating from a boat or from a fixed spot on shore can use a live-bag, and actually keep their fish alive until ready to clean and cook them, but the mobile angler needs portability.

A creel isn't intended to carry live fish or to be a substitute for a tackle box. Sure, if you're wading a hotspot and taking fish in pretty quick order, a creel will hold your catch for you, but as soon as the action ends and you go back to shore, clean those fish and put them back in the creel on a layer of ferns or clean grass. The creel's construction allows air to flow around the fish, the fern lining will hold

Broken-out pieces such as you can see at the bottom of the creel in the picture can be restored by splicing in a length of ⅛-inch dowel.

moisture, and your catch will be in good shape when cooking time rolls around.

A willow creel should be kept varnished and washed free of fish slime after it's been used. Every three or four years the varnish should be renewed. Eventually, the knocks a creel takes combined with honorable age will cause some of its willows to break, but this can be repaired. The mend will be inconspicuous if done properly.

To splice a gap such as the one you can see at the bottom right part of the creel pictured, you'll need lengths of small dowel and brown twine, a curved upholsterer's needle, a few drops of varnish, and a knife of some sort. A craft knife fitted with a sharp new blade is your best choice.

In a creel made from full-round willow twigs, a ⅛-inch dowel (available at any lumberyard) is almost the exact diameter of the willows. Measure the gap to be filled, and cut a piece of dowel just a bit

216

longer than you will need. Dunk the dowel in boiling water for about ten minutes; this will make the wood soft and pliable and it will hold this flexibility for about twenty minutes, long enough for you to complete the splice.

Taper the end of the broken willow as shown in the picture, and make a mating tapered cut on one end of the dowel. Fit the dowel into place, interweaving it into the creel to fill the gap left by the lost willow piece. The dowel should be woven in so that it will meet the broken end on the other side of the gap, and these two ends cut to overlap in a tapered joint like the one just cut.

Thread the curved needle and tie a small loop in the long end of the twine; you'll only need a length of twine about 8 to 10 inches long. Push the needle through the gap above or below the point where the tapered ends of willow and dowel overlap, starting the needle inside the creel. Pass the needle through the loop in the twine and pull tight. Now, use the needle to apply a smooth wrap of twine as shown, over

Taper the end of the broken willow piece by cutting as shown; the cut should be about ½ inch long. Make a matching tapered cut on one end of the dowel.

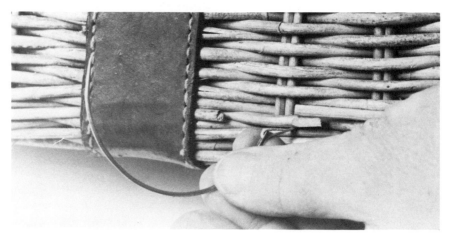

Fit the dowel into place by interweaving it in the same way the missing section was woven into the creel, and overlap the tapered end with that of the willow. You can now get an accurate measurement and taper the willow end and dowel end at the other side of the splice.

the splice and extending for about ¼ inch on either side. You can use a straight needle, or even a loop of wire, to handle the thread.

When the wrapping is complete, tie the twine off inside the creel with half hitches or a weaver's knot and cut it off. Repeat the wrapping

Using a curved upholsterer's needle threaded with light twine, begin to wrap the tapered ends of the willow and dowel.

By passing the needle alternately through the gaps above and below the splice you can make a neat wrap such as this. The text gives tying-off details.

on the other end of the splice, then varnish over the wrapping twine inside and out.

If you're working with a split-willow or rattan creel, use 50-pound test monofilament in a brown shade that will match the willow, and don't try to cut tapers in the material, just overlap the ends and wrap with thread, then varnish. In a short splice the heavy mono will be stiff enough to hold its place in a rattan or split-willow creel, which is woven more closely than a creel made of full-round willows.

One of the most frequent repair jobs a willow creel needs is the replacement of the straps that hold the top in place. Constant wetting and drying weaken the leather fast, and no dressing helps much. These straps are held in place by fasteners much like the old brass paper fasteners that staples made obsolete. Narrow blades of thin brass are held together by the head of the fastener, and usually pass through a slit washer inside the creel, where they are spread apart. The first step in replacing a strap is to feel inside the creel for the arms of the fastener and squeeze them together. Then, use pliers to pull them through to the outside.

Most shoe repair shops stock or will cut a strap of the proper width for you. Pierce the strap at the center and fit it with the buckle, as pictured. Fold the strap back on itself and pierce matching holes for the fastener. Use an ice pick or thin screwdriver blade to push the ends of the strap into place under the leather trim. Replace the fastener and spread its blades by reaching inside the creel, then pierce a hole in the upper strap to accept the tongue of the buckle.

Live-bags made of mesh can often be rewoven when breaks occur, using braided casting line of the proper size. Wire live-bags of the folding type can seldom be repaired if they are badly bent or crushed, and will have to be replaced.

An enterprising statistician once figured out that the average angler owns 3⅓ tackle boxes, one of which he uses. I'm looking forward to seeing a fisherman carrying one-third of a tackle box; I'll follow him and pick up the lures and other gear he drops. Maybe that figure isn't so illogical after all—I've got three tackle boxes and a

Put the buckle on the strap, double the strap around the crosspiece, and pierce both ends at the same time to make an opening through which the fastener will pass.

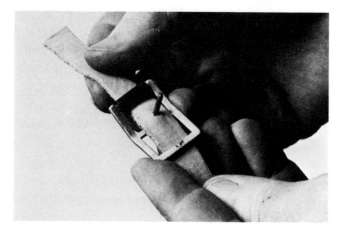

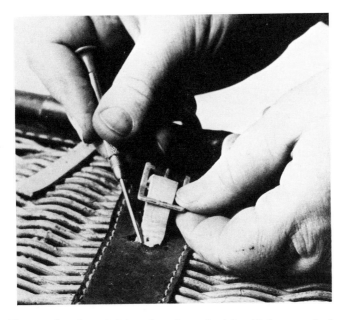

Your awl or ice pick is a handy tool with which to push the ends of the strap under the leather trim band.

Replace the fastener, spread it by reaching inside the creel.

Fit the top strap and punch the hole the newly placed buckle requires.

pocket lure box plus a few fly boxes that I suppose would equal the one-third of a tackle box the statistician cited. I suspect every fisherman is similarly equipped; most of my friends have several tackle boxes, at least one of which is so big and so heavily loaded that it can't be lifted.

High-impact plastics have just about replaced the old metal tackle box, which had a bad habit of rusting out around the hinges and in the corners. The new generation of tackle boxes don't rust, but they do pop tray rivets. These rivets can be replaced if you have the gun required to fit them, or can borrow one from a friend. Pop rivets can also be used to replace hinges and latches on metal boxes, and, combined with epoxy-coated sheet metal, can be used to repair a crack in a plastic or metal box.

Some plastics can be mended with a solvent that softens the edges of a crack and in effect reconstitutes the material on either side of a crack. Fiberglass boxes can be repaired with the same kind of kit mentioned earlier. If all else fails, try one of the "miracle adhesives" but remember not to touch your fingers to anything on which you've put these glues during a mending job.

Cutlery

The most important accessories a fisherman needs are his knives and clippers. Some fishermen don't carry clippers, depending on a knife to trim leader and lines, but I find a clipper one of the handiest tackle-box items around.

Almost every tackle store has special angler's clippers, which usually have such extras as a disgorger that's too short to be useful and a reamer for hook eyes that's too coarse for small hooks. Fingernail clippers from the dime store do all the jobs a clipper's needed for and cost less than these "angler's pals." When their edges rust out, throw them away and replace them, there's no way they can be salvaged.

Knives are another matter. A knife is an extension of its users' fingers, and familiarity with its characteristics is all-important. That's why I haven't replaced the fishing knives I've used for years. Breaking in a new one, learning how to hold it, and using it until cutting becomes an automatic matter is just too much of a job. If you haven't yet found a fishing knife that satisfies you, one with which you're completely comfortable, check out several types until you run into one that suits your hands and style of use. I still think that the best knife-blade metal is high-carbon drop-forged steel. Even though modern tungsten stainless steel can be hardened to the Rockwell C45–50 range, none of the scores of stainless steel knives I've tried has taken or held an edge like high-carbon steel.

Whatever kind of fishing knife you use, do it and yourself a favor and keep it away from that combination electric can opener/knife sharpener that's probably in your kitchen. The wheels on these things create enough heat to draw the temper from the blade of a knife being sharpened on it.

A typical cleaning knife such as the one at the bottom of the photo will have a sturdy blade with a short-arc tip. A fillet knife, shown at the top, should have a longer blade with a smoothly tapering tip.

If you do a lot of filleting, you'll want two fishing knives. Filleting and cleaning knives perform different functions and require differently shaped blades. For cleaning, you'll want a knife with a blade 4 to 6 inches long, with a short-arc tip and enough backbone to allow you to bear down when you're cutting through the spine of a fish while taking off its head and tail. For filleting, your knife should be 7 to 8 inches long, with a thin, taper-tip blade. Knives with typical shapes for each job are shown in the picture.

An accident to my favorite cleaning knife many years ago saves me a lot of effort when cleaning fish. I'd dropped the knife on a rock while cleaning a mess of trout at streamside, and the rock had chipped out a nick near the tip. I finished the job without stopping to resharpen the knife, and while I was working through the trout found that the nick in the blade provided me with an instant depth gauge for slitting a fish's belly without going too deep and tearing into the entrails. Instead of grinding out the nick, I later trued up its edges and sharpened them with a hook-hone. When I lost the original knife in a rough-water upset, I ground a similar notch in the blade of its replacement. That

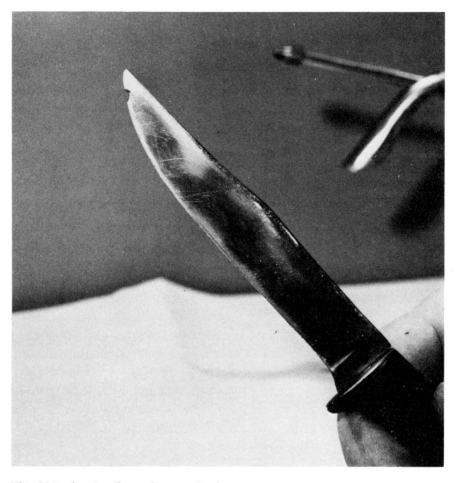

This V in the tip of my cleaning knife gives an automatic depth gauge when slitting a fish's belly. The V is kept sharp with a hook hone.

little V in the tip of the blade doesn't interfere in any way with the knife's normal use, and certainly saves worry about cutting too deeply when opening a fish.

Even the best knife in the world isn't worth much unless it's kept sharp. Cleaning knives and filleting knives should be sharpened by different techniques. Both require a major sharpening two or three times a year, starting them on a medium-grit Carborundum or silicon carbide stone and finishing them on a soft Arkansas or Washita stone. Between major sharpenings, the Arkansas stone should be used occasionally to keep the blades razor-sharp.

When sharpening the cleaning knife, push the blade forward on the stone starting at the tip and going along the arc of the blade to its straight portion. Hold the blade at an angle of about 20 to 25 degrees in relation to the stone while pushing it forward, and keep the stone well oiled. Turn the blade from one side to the other and make about eight to ten pushing passes on each side, then with the blade still being held at the same angle, oscillate it on the stone on both sides for a minute or two. This gives you a broad V-edge, which is what you want for hard cutting.

A filleting knife should have a narrow V-edge. Sharpen it by oscillating the edge on the stone on alternate sides while holding the blade at an angle of 8 to 10 degrees in relation to the stone. The edge of a filleting knife, which is used in stroking cuts, shouldn't be obviously slanted in its relationship to the blade.

There are a lot of angling accessories that this chapter doesn't even pretend to cover. Most of them are things like folding landing nets, depth thermometers, and gadgets designed to tie knots in leader material. None of them really contributes much to a fisherman except pride of ownership, and if you're like most anglers you'd rather be proud of the number and size of the fish you hook instead of the number and cost of the gadgets you hang on yourself.

APPENDIX

The following lists should steer you to sources of product information and repairs for most fishing tackle, as well as providing sources of materials and tools needed by tackle-tinkerers.

General Tackle Manufacturers

General tackle manufacturers do not sell direct to customers but market their products through retail outlets nationwide. All these firms have factory repair shops, and their repair service includes selling replacement parts through their Customer Service Departments. Your inquiries should be addressed to these departments.

Aladdin Laboratories   Automatic fly reels
620 South 8th Street
Minneapolis, Minnesota 55101

Berkley & Co.   Rods, reels, lines
Spirit Lake, Louisiana 51360

Browning   Rods, outdoor accessories
Box 500
Morgan, Utah 84050

Daiwa Corp. 14011 South Normandie Gardena, California 90247	Rods, reels, lines
Fenwick 14799 Chestnut Street Westminster, California 92683	Rods
Garcia Corp. 110 Charlotte Place Englewood Cliffs, New Jersey 07632	Rods, reels, lines, lures, accessories
Gladding Corp. 441 Stuart Street Boston, Massachusetts 02116	Rods, reels, lines, lures, accessories
James Heddon's Sons 414 West Street Dowagiac, Michigan 49047	Rods, reels, lures
Johnson Reels Co. Johnson Park Mankato, Minnesota 56001	Reels
Kodiak Co. Box 467 Ironwood, Michigan 49938	Rods
H. L. Leonard Rod Co. Box 393 Central Valley, New York 10917	Rods
Martin Reel Co. 30 East Main Street Mohawk, New York 13407	Rods, reels, lines, lures, accessories
Orvis 10 River Road Manchester, Vermont 05254	Rods, reels, accessories
Penn Fishing Tackle Co. 3028 West Hunting Park Avenue Philadelphia, Pennsylvania 19132	Reels
Pflueger Sporting Goods Co. 301 Ansin Boulevard Hallandale, Florida 33009	Rods, reels, lines, accessories

Quick Corporation of America 620 Terminal Way Costa Mesa, California 92627	Rods, reels, lines
Scientific Anglers 3M Center St. Paul, Minnesota 55101	Rods, reels, lines
Shakespeare Co. Box 246 Columbia, South Carolina 29202	Rods, reels, lines, lures, accessories
St. Croix Rod Co. 9909 South Shore Drive Minneapolis, Minnesota 55441	Rods
True Temper Corporation 1623 Euclid Avenue Cleveland, Ohio 44115	Rods, reels, lines, accessories
Wright & McGill, Inc. 4245 East 46th Avenue Denver, Colorado 80216	Rods, reels, hooks
Zebco 6101 East Apache Tulsa, Oklahoma 74101	Rods, reels, lures

Specialty Manufacturers

Specialty manufacturers produce components or limited lines of tackle. These customarily sell through retailers, but if you have trouble locating their products they will furnish you the names of outlets near you.

Allan Tackle Manufacturing Co. 325 Duffy Avenue Hicksville, New York 11802	Guides, rod fittings
Auto-Gaff 4 Reynolds Street East Providence, Rhode Island 02914	Automatic gaffs

Cortland Line Co. 67 East Court Street Cortland, New York 13045	Lines
Featherweight Products 3456 Ocean View Boulevard Glendale, California 91208	Rod components, lures
Gudebrod Bros. 12 South 12th Street Philadelphia, Pennsylvania 19107	Lines, rod winding threads, rod finishes, guides, lures
Varmac Manufacturing Co. 4201 Redwood Avenue Los Angeles, California 90066	Guides

Suppliers

Suppliers specialize in mail-order sale of tackle, its components, and tackle-tinkering tools. These firms usually issue catalogs, and the prices of their catalogs are given as part of their listing.

Angler's Pro Shop Box 35 Springfield, Ohio 45501	Rod and lure components.
Brookstone Co. 121 Vose Farm Road Peterborough, New Hampshire 03458	Not a tackle supplier, but has hard-to-find tools, adhesives, useful to tackle-tinkerers.
Clemens Custom Rods Box 850A, Route 2 Wescosville, Pennsylvania 18106	Rod components. Free catalog.
Coren's Rod & Reel Service 6619 North Clark Street Chicago, Illinois 60626	Rod and lure components.
Herter's, Inc. Waseca, Minnesota 56093	Rod and lure components, tools. Catalog, $1.00, refundable.
E. Hille Box 269 Williamsport, Pennsylvania 17701	Rod and lure components. Free catalog.

Limit Tackle Co.
Box 369
Richardson, Texas 75080

Rod and lure components. Catalog, 25¢.

Midland Tackle Co.
66 Route 17
Sloatsburg, New York 10974

Rod and lure components. Catalog, 25¢.

Netcraft Co.
3101 Sylvania Avenue
Toledo, Ohio 43613

Rod and lure components. Free catalog.

Reed Tackle Co.
Box 390
Caldwell, New Jersey 07006

Rod and lure components. Catalog, 50¢.

Roy System Shoes
26 Broadway
Denver, Colorado 80203

Waders, wading sandals, felt soles and installation.

Fritz von Schlegell
1409 Santa Fe Avenue
Los Angeles, California 90021

Waders, boots, felt sole kits, fishing clothing.

INDEX